# THE
# END

### WHAT JESUS _REALLY_ SAID
### ABOUT THE LAST THINGS

# A.J.CONYERS

**InterVarsity Press**
Downers Grove, Illinois

*InterVarsity Press® is the book-publishing division of InterVarsity Christian Fellowship®, a student movement active on campus at hundreds of universities, colleges and schools of nursing in the United States of America, and a member movement of the International Fellowship of Evangelical Students. For information about local and regional activities, write Public Relations Dept., InterVarsity Christian Fellowship, 6400 Schroeder Rd., P.O. Box 7895, Madison, WI 53707-7895.*

*All Scripture quotations, unless otherwise indicated, are taken from the HOLY BIBLE, NEW INTERNATIONAL VERSION®. NIV®. Copyright © 1973, 1978, 1984 by International Bible Society. Used by permission of Zondervan Publishing House. All rights reserved.*

*Cover photograph: Paul Berger/Tony Stone Images*
*ISBN 0-8308-1617-8*

*Printed in the United States of America* ♾

**Library of Congress Cataloging-in-Publication Data**

*Conyers, A. J., 1944-*
    *The end: what Jesus really said about the Last Things/A. J. Conyers.*
        *p.    cm.*
    *Includes bibliographical references.*
    *ISBN 0-8308-1617-8 (alk. paper)*
    *1. Jesus Christ—Views on eschatology.   2. Bible. N.T. Mark XIII—Criticism, interpretation, etc.   3. Eschatology—Biblical teaching.   4. Eschatology.   I. Title.*
    *BS2417.E7C66   1995*
    *236'.09'015—dc20*                                    *95-32672*
                                                          *CIP*

| 17 | 16 | 15 | 14 | 13 | 12 | 11 | 10 | 9 | 8 | 7 | 6 | 5 | 4 | 3 | 2 | 1 |
|----|----|----|----|----|----|----|----|----|----|----|----|----|----|----|----|----|
| 09 | 08 | 07 | 06 | 05 | 04 | 03 | 02 | 01 | 00 | 99 | 98 | 97 | 96 | 95 | | |

*To Katie Addison Gilbert*

# Introduction
# Apocalypse Today?

*O*NLY DAYS BEFORE THE MOST DECISIVE AND REMEMBERED event in history—Jesus' execution on a Roman cross—he was teaching disciples about signs and events of the end times.

Biblical scholars often dispute the full authenticity of what we have of those teachings. It is almost certain that we do not have all of them. But what we do have in the "Olivet discourse" of Mark 13, along with parallel passages in Matthew and Luke, was for many centuries the center of Christian reflection on the end of world history. These passages give us, moreover, some of the clearest teachings on the "last things" (the doctrine of *eschatology*) that appear anywhere in Scripture.

In modern times, much of Christian eschatology has involved interpreting the concept of the kingdom of God, asking how we should understand Jesus' anticipation of its arrival, or looking at Christ's return vis-à-vis the "millennium" of Revelation 20. So we wind up reading these richly suggestive teachings of Jesus, taken from that critical period before his supreme act on our behalf, under the influence of interpretations that have little to do with the text itself.

This book hopes to recover for the thoughtful reader, and not just for the theologically trained, something of the directness and practicability that was once found in Mark 13 and its parallels. Along with that, I hope the reader recaptures a sense of its power to address the real fears and aspirations of the human heart. Perhaps this is *our* critical time in history; at the least, it is a time of crisis in many lives. In any case, we need to rescue these teachings from the overlayers of refined interpretations—whether "realized eschatology" or "premillennialism" or any other refinement imported from elsewhere in Scripture—that have come to be an assortment of tails with which to wag the dog. It is the dog we are interested in here, though we'll allow others to affix the appropriate millennial tail.

I would certainly not deny the importance of making theological judgments based on a broader reading of Scripture. But it seems to me that there might be value, at least occasionally, in holding back the traditional questions and categories of eschatological interpretation just long enough to hear the words of the Olivet discourse itself. Just perhaps we can understand what Jesus said about the end time better if we ignore for the moment those modes of thought that have long since pigeonholed discussion on this subject, and if instead we sit quietly with Peter and Andrew, James and John, listening intently to the words that Jesus said would "never pass away."

I propose that we do so by taking Mark 13 as the spine of this study, glancing to the right and left at the parallels in Matthew and Luke, and occasionally even focusing on one of these other Gospels (as in chapter three) when the topic we've undertaken seems to require it. In the end you will see that we've explored the most important of the Gospel records on Jesus' apocalyptic teachings, beginning with the first verse of Mark 13 and following through to the last verse. My hope is that this study proves to help the reader refocus on some really fundamental Christian principles as much as it helped the writer.

I've had some excellent assistance along the way, especially from the always reliable insights of my editor at InterVarsity Press, Rodney Clapp, and from my wife, Debbie, whose comments on each chapter combined the temperament of a scholar and the sympathies of a devoted wife. I have benefited from the careful reading and valuable suggestions of my young colleague and intern David Roof. The staff of the Mendel Rivers Library at Charleston Southern University also came to my aid on many occasions, especially Margaret Gilmore, Sandra Hughes, Jim Lowe and Barbara Anderson.

Finally, I am grateful to Cadwallader and Lucy Jones for the use of their wonderful beach house—the one that often sheltered Francis and Edith Schaeffer—as I put the finish on these chapters.

# 1

# Facing
# the Question

*I* KNEW THE DREADED QUESTION WAS LURKING OUT THERE somewhere.

Just out of seminary, I was teaching our small Wednesday-night congregation from the Gospel of Matthew. We had come to the close-of-the-age prophecies of Jesus commonly known as the Olivet discourse, where he was answering the disciples' question "Tell us . . . when will this happen, and what will be the sign of your coming and of the end of the age?" (Mt 24:3).

All at once Mary, not unknown for speaking a millisecond or two ahead of thinking, said, "Pastor, I think we are nearer to the end of the world than ever before! What do you think?"

As I was gathering my wits in reply to this sudden burst of prophesy, we both at once caught her unintended truism and began to laugh. "Well," I said, "when it comes to prophecy, that's a safe place to begin."

Mary had gotten me off the hook. The truth is, I wanted not only to begin there, but to end there as well. I was relieved not to have to deal with such questions seriously. And I was not prepared to admit, even to myself, that questions about "the time of the end" are abundantly sensible and obvious questions in light of what is actually there in the New Testament text.

Not that I was disinterested. I was, in fact, secretly fascinated with this kind of discussion. And I knew as well that no subject aroused interest and curiosity among Christian people—and even among non-Christians—more than an investigation of these end-time prophecies. Psychologists say that using the word *death* in the title of a book increases its sales. In a similar way, and probably for the same reasons, people are intrigued by the subject of our collective end, the cosmic death that threatens all existence. It evokes awe, a fascination with that which is terrifying.

The motivation was there, I had to admit.

Still, something held me back. It was, I suppose, a sense that this was a vulgarizing of the Christian faith—the sensationalism of Bible thumpers with their charts and timetables. It was entertainment for people wanting teachers long on certainty and short on substance. These were the kinds of thoughts that ran through my mind, justifying what can only now be seen as a cowardly evasion of a self-evident question.

### Confessions of a Skeptic

On the other hand, suppose someone asks, "Well, just what do you *do* with all those allusions to the end of the age in the teachings of Jesus?"

Now, there's a question that can send serious readers of the New Testament scurrying in several directions, and some for the nearest cover. It would be impossible to guess how each reader of this book would respond. I can be sure that some of you are as skeptical as I have always been about authors and preachers who pretend to know too much about the end time. Others may come to a book such as this with end-time itineraries already well fixed in their minds. Some will be reluctant to admit their interest (for reasons I'd like to explore in a moment), and others will have a natural and open curiosity.

Let me tell you how my own attitude toward this subject has changed over the years. I want to do this first, so I can invite you to think about some of the most extraordinary truths—all relating to the end time—that are conveyed in the Christian gospel. I hope that by the end of this chapter at least, you will be neither put off by the subject itself nor so intent on one way of thinking about the end time that you fail to hear something important that the apostles heard from Jesus.

## Doomsayers and Polite Society

I remember walking down an Atlanta street with my mother and seeing something quite shocking. I was old enough to read but too young to judge the social inappropriateness of what I saw. An old man trudged back and forth on the sidewalk. Wild white hair frizzed out from beneath an olive-colored slouch hat. An unkempt beard lapped over a sign hanging from his neck—a sign that said, "The End Is Near."

"How does he know?" I asked my mother, naively expecting that an old man thus occupied must have good reason for spending his day on the streets of Atlanta.

"He doesn't," she answered. Something in my mother's quick reply told me that such people were not to be taken seriously. The subject of "The End" somehow was associated in her mind (and in mine) with those outside the pale of trustworthy society. Later I saw the cartoons and the comedians on TV and heard the jokes, all reinforcing the bit of social wisdom I learned that day: Those who talk about the end, those who parade with their sandwich signs announcing doom, are not to be taken seriously. And anyone who takes up that subject seriously is at least running the risk of being associated with those old men, those ultimate misfits, announcing doom on the streets of modern cities, where all sensible people ignore them.

Later something would happen to help me break the habit of lumping together all kinds of interest in the last things. But even in my seminary and graduate school days, I would not be aware of what exactly kept me from dealing freely with both my own fascination and the huge segments of the Bible that address this subject. The intuition persisted that something was wrong, something was just a bit shameful and reprehensible, about the subject of the end time.

### The Education of a Confirmed Anti-apocalypticist

My studies in college and graduate school only confirmed this sense that eschatology (the doctrine of the last things) was a fertile ground for every misspent human expectation. History had provided abundant reason to be suspicious of doomsday predictions and adventist movements of various kinds. The chiliasts—from the Greek word for "thousand"—have shown up in every age since the spread of Christianity began. They expected a millennial (thousand-year) new age, something profoundly disruptive bringing the old world to an end.

Montanists in the second century fully expected the New Jerusalem to descend literally from heaven onto Phrygian soil. Even one of the greatest theologians of the West, Tertullian, wrote of a walled city seen in the sky above Jerusalem early every morning for forty days. Like people throughout the world, the great Tertullian was swept along in eschatological excitement.

Obviously he, and the others, were deluded.

But the delusion was far from innocent. The dream of the millennium wound into the early Crusades, raising in the popular imagination a picture of a Christ who desires a mighty army wielding bloody swords against infidels. It was to be found among the medieval flagellants who inflicted tortures on themselves in expectation of avoiding God's imminent judgment. In the thirteenth century, hopes and apocalyptic anxieties were fueled by the prophecies of Joachim of Fiore, who taught the arrival of a new age of the Spirit. Huge bands of men and boys, usually led by a priest, would march in candlelit procession from town to town in northern Italy, gathering in the town square, where they would proceed to flog themselves hour after hour. The effect of these grim flagellants was astounding—masses of penitents would follow them, swelling their number for procession to the next city. Even the great feuding parties of the Guelphs and Ghibellines in Italy were interrupted in their protracted warfare.

**Millennial Madness**
The new age would be better and of a higher order than the last. The baptism of water was replaced by a baptism of blood. The flagellants imagined that an angel watched over them—an angel named Venus, who oversaw the "wedding" preparation as they "dressed" themselves in the red garment of their own blood.[1]

This madness broke out again north of the Alps in the fourteenth century, spurred on by the Black Death. What had begun as a misguided *imitatio Christi* began to turn dark and ugly. Mobs fastened on Jews as "poisoners of wells." What followed, mixed with end-time expectations, was the cruelest and largest annihilation of Jews until the twentieth century. Some church clerics dropped out of the movement, to be replaced by the "radical priests" of medieval Europe, wielding the sword to liberate the world of evil. New age expectations left no room for moderation, much less for the life-honoring piety that the pope begged for as Germany and Low Country towns were ravaged and the Jewish population depleted.

In the late 1340s flagellant expectations of the end reached a fever pitch. The Black Death, earthquakes in Italy and corruption in the church—all spelled the days of antichrist and the end. As Norman

Cohn points out, "It is no coincidence that it was in these years that the most famous of the German Antichrist-plays were composed and performed."[2]

These prophets of the new age sometimes tired of basking in the light of a glorious new day and desired instead, like Konrad Schmid of Thuringia, to *be* the light. A layman well versed in the traditions of the flagellant movement, Schmid regarded himself as the true bearer of the new age. Proclaiming himself king of Thuringia (central Germany), he became associated in the public mind with a mythical notion of a resurrected emperor who was to fulfill Isaiah's prophecies. Followers were told to submit utterly to his will, to be "as soft and yielding as silk" in his hands. He continued to inflame the countryside with his pronouncements of judgment, doom and a new age, until in 1368 he announced that the last judgment would occur in the following year and the millennium would then commence. By then the church and the civil authorities had begun to take measures against him, and as quickly as the bizarre movement arose, it disappeared.

But the pattern was to be repeated many times, in many places: Thomas Münzer and the Peasant Revolt, the Münster Anabaptist revolt led by John of Leiden, the Taborites of Bohemia and many others.

Each responded to injustices. Münzer rightly pointed out the hardships and economic burdens of the poor. He gathered peasants for war under a banner emblazoned with a rainbow, sign of apocalyptic judgment and God's protection to the faithful. Jan Bockelson, or John of Leiden as he is also called, railed along with other militant Anabaptists against church officials who loved the world too much.

Each expected apocalyptic events to turn the world upside down and establish a new order. Münzer announced the certain intervention of God against the proud and mighty, ushering in what was prophesied in Ezekiel 34 and Matthew 24 and the day of wrath of Revelation 6. The Taborites regarded themselves as "avenging angels of God and warriors of Christ" ready to kill the "evil ones" (the unconverted) in anticipation of the millennium of Christ. The militant Anabaptists anticipated messianic woes, signs of the new kingdom, and announced their messiah in John of Leiden. All looked for the end to rescue them from the present; all foresaw the imminent kingdom of God; all had forsaken a dying world to follow the promise of a dawning new age; all were accompanied by signs and wonders.

But furthermore, all of these apocalyptic prophets, without exception, fell into traps of pride to the point of self-deification, cruelty to the point of the demonic, and moral license on the order of a Sodom and Gomorrah. Münzer imagined himself a Gideon who would catch cannonballs in the sleeves of his cloak; John of Leiden imagined himself a Christ who would end thievery by becoming the only thief. Münzer called for slaughter and got it: over 100,000 peasants were lost. John of Leiden demanded obedience, draining the city of Münster of every available private fund of money ("true Christians should have no money," he said) and executing men and women without trial on the basis of a flash of suspicion. He threw elaborate banquets after which an enemy would be brought from prison and beheaded for his satisfaction. While his captive city was under siege and starving, he lived in a sumptuous style, reasoning that for those dead to the flesh and the world any pleasure was permitted.[3] He initiated polygamous marriage and permitted himself a harem of over a hundred women, thus proving how detached he was from the allurements of the flesh, the world and the devil.

### The Gnostic Crisis of Modern Times

I learned that there were other reasons to suspect the endless procession of end-time pronouncements. My early suspicions of white-haired prophets on the streets of Atlanta were now strengthened by the writings of Eric Voegelin and Gerhart Niemeyer. Both of these authors showed me how the habit of reducing New Testament expectations to an imminent expectation of some "final" state of being had exercised deadly influence on the West.

The medieval fanaticism of the militant Anabaptists, the Franciscan spirituals and the Brethren of the Free Spirit eventually took on more secular forms. Voegelin said that secularized end-time hopes were similar to the Gnostic theologizing of early Christian heresies. They created social disorder by reducing Christian hope to a this-worldly, imminent expectation. This tendency was, moreover, characteristic of certain modern mass movements, such as Nazism and communism, that wreaked havoc in the twentieth century.

Suddenly I began to see the world of public events in a more vivid and significant way. A light came on—and it illuminated what was happening in my world. From the Nazi movement with its announcement of a Third Reich (like Joachim of Fiore's "Third Age"), which it also called the Thousand-Year Reich (a millennial kingdom), to the communist movement with its expectations of revolution resulting in world peace and prosperity in a secular millennium, I began to see striking similarities with what had gone on before on the fringes of pseudo-Christianity. Modern movements, following in alarming fashion the pattern of Thomas Münzer and John of Leiden, from dreams to madness, from madness to horrible cruelty, were no longer fringe movements but were setting the fate of whole continents, murdering millions and dragging the world to the edge of an atomic abyss.

It was clear to me that the seeds of religious apocalypticism were bearing deadly fruit.

### A Myth-Spent Youth

When I was a student at Southeastern Baptist Seminary in North Carolina back in the late sixties, the faculty was reported to be heavily influenced by the theology of Rudolf Bultmann, a modern German theologian who wanted to extract the core of Christian faith from its supposed mythological shell. The rumor of the Bultmannian spell at

Southeastern was not entirely true; but it was true enough, I think, that Bultmann's demythologizing influenced some basic attitudes toward prophecy and the miraculous. I was not immune to what was already my tendency to be exceedingly skeptical, or at least publicly reticent, about any end-time speculation.

Bultmann had said that the framework of mythology undergirding New Testament assertions could no longer be supported by people today. That mythology includes the notion that this age is "held in bondage by Satan, sin, and death . . . and hastens towards its end. That end will come very soon, and will take the form of a cosmic catastrophe. It will be inaugurated by the 'woes' of the last time. Then the Judge will come from heaven, the dead will rise, the last judgement will take place, and men will enter into eternal salvation or damnation." Then he said, "This then is the mythical view of the world which the New Testament presupposes when it presents the event of redemption which is the subject of its preaching."[4]

About that same time Hal Lindsey's *The Late Great Planet Earth* was published. This popular work argued for the soon return of Christ. It met with instant success in the market (proving once again the power of this topic and the huge public interest in it), but it also provoked the academic equivalent of hoots and catcalls in theological schools such as mine.

We, after all, thought Bultmann was only speaking evident common sense when he said that expectation of the end of history was a part of the Bible's "mythical eschatology." And "as every school boy knows," he said, "[history] will continue to run its course."[5]

I might well have been content with these very respectable reservations of mine had it not been for an unforeseen circumstance. It was an event so weird, so unbelievable—and so very public—that it became for me, and I am sure for others, a bizarre, terrifying, yet powerful image of our times.

But first there were some less dramatic turns in my discovery of this subject that prepared the way, and that led to an openness to the question "Are these the last days?"—a question I would not, in an earlier day, have touched with a ten-foot pole.

Dale Moody, that unparalleled teacher of theology among Baptists, fiery, combative, never a stranger to controversy, the first Protestant theologian to teach at the Pontifical Gregorian University in Rome, a friend and theological companion of some of the great names in contemporary theology (Barth, Brunner, Tillich and others) and an Oxford scholar—in short, a man whose credentials I was bound to respect—was to be my supervisor in my pursuit of the Ph.D. He was also what he called a "historical premillennialist" who believed in the more or less literal fulfillment of the prophecies of the New Testament concerning the end of time. His book *The Hope of Glory* was a powerful marshaling of biblical teachings on the end of the age, the parousia (Christ's return, literally "appearance"), the judgment, the kingdom of God.

In short, in Louisville, Kentucky, I was forced to come face to face with an overwhelming reality. I came to realize that the subject of the "last things"—eschatology—was not optional for people who took the Bible seriously: it was not an epilogue to Christian theology (as I had often taken it to be) but was a central thrust, a theme that permeated everything, and made the gospel apply to everything, and made sense of everything. That is one of the things I want to demonstrate in this book: the central place of eschatology in Christian thought.

Furthermore, the teachings of Jesus were central in these eschatological prophecies. If only an enthusiastic later movement of Christianity had made predictions concerning the end of history, that would have been one thing. But given that Jesus himself not only included these things in his teachings but in fact talked of little else, we have a much different situation. It dawned on me that a focus on the "last things" was of ultimate importance to understanding the Christian faith.

Others besides Moody had seen this, of course. And in the sixties and seventies eschatology became an increasingly important part of theological work. I became particularly interested in the approach of one of the so-called eschatological theologians who began to dominate the theology of that period. Jürgen Moltmann and his treatment of the future-oriented or hope-oriented theme in Christianity became the subject of my dissertation. I had an opportunity to spend a semester in Germany with Moltmann, and his theology was later the subject of my book *God, Hope and History* (1988).

During this time that I was closely involved with Moltmann's theology, two things became powerfully clear to me. One is that the religion of the previous generation, even in the expressions of major theologians, had become largely a private matter. Popular religion had become for many people a "spiritual" thing; that is, it centered on the private realm of personal experience. I also was beginning to see, however, that if Jesus' teachings are in any sense to be taken seriously, we must pay attention to what his teachings on the end of history do in the realm of a "public" religion. In a word, the end of history is something that can only be the same for all of us. This expectation is shockingly communal, because it has to do with the destiny of the whole cosmos. It defies the tendency to spiritualize and privatize religion.

The second realization was even more important. We were, at the end of the twentieth century, moving toward a realization of the end time. What Bultmann said "every schoolboy" would know could no longer be taken for granted. We were becoming, around the world, a people with a sense of the apocalypse. We were living every day with the apocalyptic dangers of atomic annihilation, environmental catastrophes and the abyss of random, widespread and even universal destruction. This had never happened before. Now we thought not only of our own death but of the possible death of humanity.

These dreads may at times have been overdone. But they were there.

And we all know that for the first time in world history, there are good technical reasons to contemplate the possibility of the earth's destruction. But, of course, it is reassuring to know that the world by and large wants to live and is not given to the irrational excesses of self-destruction. Or—do we know that?

### The Face of Self-Destruction

This last question brings me to that "weird, shocking and very public" event I mentioned earlier. In the summer of 1978 something inexpressibly tragic happened to some Americans on foreign soil. This event has been often mentioned since that time, but it is seldom lingered over or analyzed. It was the Jim Jones affair: an Indiana minister led his large flock on an odyssey that ended in mass suicide in the jungles of Guyana.

Like many a messiah before him, whether Lenin or Münzer, Jones dreamed of justice and equality. Like the flagellants, he was obsessed by an apocalypse—only this time a modern technological apocalypse. He led his followers to "Jonestown," the place that, ironically, he calculated to be the safest place on earth. In an uncanny repeat of Münster nearly five centuries earlier, he demanded everything from his followers, lived in self-indulgent license and led the people to self-annihilation.

For months the sad images filled TV screens, hanging over the landscape of our national consciousness like an alien moon—weird beyond words, yet shedding an uncanny light on our modern experience with its self-proclaimed freedom, its self-conscious modernity, its abundance and its unalienable death wish.

How could I have ever believed that human behavior is mostly governed by reason? I was quite sure the notion didn't come from specific examples of human behavior. Not even my own. The Jonestown tragedy left me with a strong impression that there is something powerful at work in history, and in human life, and it cannot be altogether or satisfactorily described as reason.

The powerful fascination of religion comes prior to reason. It is the fascination of a crisis, the fascination of a very simple and ultimate decision that bears within it human destiny. At some point we really do make an ultimate choice—an eschatological choice—and it has to do with the last things. Or, we could say, it is a choice to live or to die. The Jones cult stared into that abyss and chose death.

I began to see that the street-walking doomsayers, the flagellants, the Jan Bockelsons and the modern apocalypticists of the secular type—the Stalins and the Hitlers—were only at a very superficial level bringing discredit to New Testament expectations of the last days. In fact, in a much more significant way they were confirming what had been said long ago, when Jesus linked sin to judgment yet promised the ultimate triumph of God, when he taught that the path any man or woman takes leads to an end and can be understood only in light of the end.

If I ever doubted it, I came to realize later that faith is not one thing among many in life. It is a choice. The paths of life sort themselves out in two directions ultimately—not like spokes on a wheel but like the dual directions of a single decision, up or down, in or out, yes or no, for or against. "This day I call heaven and earth as witnesses against you that I have set before you life and death, blessings and curses. Now choose life, so that you and your children may live" (Deut 30:19).

The choice is not ultimately Christ or something else, some other way. It is Christ and antichrist. And antichrist is never indifferent to the real Christ or to the reality of God's kingdom. Should it surprise us that in the evolution of choices, what we earlier thought of as varied and many-faceted becomes finally simple and direct—that it ultimately becomes a religious choice, a yes or a no to God?

For me, the doctrine of the last things was no longer a mélange of disconnected prophecies, remote from our time and without connection to the other things Jesus taught. Like a stream filling the banks of my mind, things began to flow together that had hitherto been the stationary shores on which I could live a generally secular life, detached from the stream of "religion" and "theology" that constituted my career and my church life. I began to see that the teachings of Jesus centered on a very few prophetic utterances. And furthermore, these utterances speak to *our* time in a way more significant than the date-setters and speculators ever guessed.

# 2

# Not One
# Stone Left

*As [Jesus] was leaving the temple,*
*one of his disciples said to him,*
*"Look, Teacher! What massive stones!*
*What magnificent buildings!"*

*"Do you see all these great buildings?"*
*replied Jesus. "Not one stone*
*here will be left on another;*
*every one will be thrown down."*

*(MARK 13:1-2)*

*I*T WAS SPRING. PASSOVER WAS APPROACHING IN THE THIRteenth year after Joseph, called Caiaphas, was made high priest. A young rabbi and his disciples walked unhurriedly out of the midday shadows of a temple gateway. One of the group appeared slightly older than the Rabbi himself. Strands of gray lightened his beard but had not yet touched the raven-colored hair of his head. This older one walked down the steps, followed by others who were still in animated conversation with the Rabbi.

One lingered behind. His eyes moved slowly from the Roman eagle spreading its sculpted wings over the gateway to the disciples moving down the steps. The eagle was offensive to many Jews, who considered it both a pagan image and a sign of foreign domination. One could not tell whether the singularly dark expression on the man's face was for the eagle or for the group of Jews ahead of him on the steps. He tugged sharply at the heavy leather purse laced to his belt and walked on.

Had we been there, we certainly could not have detected the drama unfolding now—a drama taking place at this instant on the level of the human heart, one that would in a matter of days erupt on the streets of Jerusalem. It was a drama that, as the Rabbi would shortly tell his disciples, must one day engulf the world.

As they left the temple, disciples expressed astonishment at the most recent evidences of Herod's rebuilding, a project of temple enlargement that Herod the Great had begun some fifty years earlier. "Look, Teacher!" one of them said. "What massive stones! What magnificent buildings!" (Mk 13:1).

Jesus' reply to this remark foreshadowed the crisis to come and, one might say, all of the crises yet to come. It portended the approaching day of Jesus' death, the days of Jerusalem's destruction some forty years later and the day when no one would escape the general crisis of the world itself. "Do you see all these great buildings?" he said. "Not one stone here will be left on another; every one will be thrown down" (v. 2).

This brief exchange between Jesus and his disciples in Mark 13 (and paralleled in Matthew 24 and Luke 21) begins one of the New Testament's most extraordinary teachings. It is the longest explicitly eschatological teaching—that is, teaching on the "last things"—that the Gospel writers give us from the life of Jesus.

It seems that the continuation of this discussion did not take place, however, until Jesus was on the Mount of Olives, opposite the temple, with only four disciples. The four included the older one and his brother, Peter and Andrew; and another pair of brothers, James and John. These four had been with him from the beginning. They composed his closest circle of friends. It was only then that they asked him what must have been stirring in their minds from the very moment he startled them with these words about the temple's destruction.

Mark tells us who was there. Matthew recalls for us the full import of the question: "Tell us . . . when will this happen, and what will be

the sign of your coming and of the end of the age?"
The word translated "age" here is *aiōn* (eon); and what lies behind
this word, closer to the idiom of these Palestinian Jews, was the Hebrew word *'ôlām,* which is translated either "world" or "age." So the
disciples were not thinking of a mere transition in time (as we would
think of an age, as in "the age of faith"); "the end of the age" implied
something of a catastrophic nature. It suggested the end of the world
itself.

In this question, however, are two matters that should arrest our
attention. The first is a point that I must wait until later to explore
fully, but that I want simply to mention here in anticipation. It is a
key element in Jesus' apocalyptic teachings. That is, Jesus and his
disciples were focusing on an as-yet-unfulfilled crisis. I am using the
term *crisis* in the sense of the Greek from which we have borrowed
the word. It means "judgment" and derives from the word meaning
"to decide," to choose or discriminate between one thing and another.
Jesus always spoke of the "end of the age" in terms of a *crisis,* a
judgment both from the standpoint of God's action toward humanity
and of our action in response to him.

In Jesus' teachings on the Mount of Olives, the crisis is seen on
several levels. Jesus has now made his appearance to Jerusalem. His
messianic claim has been revealed. Now, on the Mount of Olives, he
retreats with his disciples, leaving Jerusalem to its own crisis—its own
decision. In the meantime he faces an impending crisis; and, knowing
this, he places this moment in the stream of events leading to crises
yet to come: the destruction of Jerusalem and the temple, wars and
rumors of wars, persecutions, and finally the great judgment at the end
of the age.

### The Temple and the Cosmos
We will return to this key idea of "crisis." But there is something else
in this discussion that immediately takes us by surprise. It is the ap-

parent leap from "the end of the temple" to "the end of the world." Why is it that, apparently, both Jesus and his disciples moved easily and inevitably from the thought of one to the thought of the other? Why did they make such an association? We will consider, step by step, what it was in their experience that brought these subjects together so strongly in their minds.

Once we grasp this connection, we hold a second important key to Jesus' teachings on the end of the world. Let's explore this connection first; it will help us when we return to the idea of "crisis."

There were several reasons for the immediate association that the disciples made between the temple's end and the world's end. I will move from the most obvious and least important to the most important and least apparent.

**The Temple in Time and Eternity**
First, nothing could have appeared more permanent to those Galilean disciples, in from the north country, than this enlarged temple that Herod had under construction. He intended to impress the Jews with this pious project, and the world with a public structure larger than the Roman Forum. He spared no expense, no effort.

Even the unfinished building strikes the disciples with awe. Here lies a column, one of thirty belonging to a portico. It is thirty-seven and a half feet long—and all of one stone. There stand single stones, twenty to forty feet in length, weighing more than a hundred tons. Already for fifty years workers have labored on this project, and a quarter of a century later they still will not be finished. After all, this is a building for the ages—a monument of permanence in the midst of a sea of change. Just as the Herods will always reign, and as the Caesars will rule the world, so this temple will greet pilgrims from far-flung lands over endless generations.

I should stress, however, that the sentiment I am describing was not merely a recognition of the immense size of the temple. The feeling that people in ancient Palestine had for this place is perhaps better captured by the word *grandeur*. The whole effect of the building, with its massive dimensions, with the gleaming white marble walls of the sanctuary standing at one end of spacious paved courtyards, with bright gilded castings along the capitals and eaves, was bound to impress people with its splendor, giving rise to a sense of awe. Jews of the first century did not hesitate to call this wondrous structure "famous throughout the world" (2 Maccabees 2:22 NRSV). Not only the sight of it but even the smell impressed visitors. Aromatic spices emanating from the temple "caused goats to sneeze for miles around."[1] Josephus described the amazement with which pilgrims would react to the polished white stone of the building, even from a considerable distance.[2]

We can only imagine the thrill and sense of anticipation as pilgrims approached this luminous spot in ancient times, whether at night in a torchlit procession or in the daytime with chants of psalms and the waving of palm branches. From the testimony of many contemporary witnesses, we have the clear impression that the whole atmosphere of such a place and structure seemed unlike anything on earth.

It was at least partly this feeling of grandeur associated with the very physical aspects of the temple itself that caused minds to move easily from "the destruction of the temple" to "the end of the world." Any catastrophe that would end the temple must necessarily be of a magnitude to topple the world as well. It was much as Romans felt about the massive sports arena in the midst of their city. For centuries they repeated this saying:

As long as the colosseum stands
Rome will stand.
When the colosseum falls
Rome will fall.
When Rome falls
The world will fall.

Yet the stunning appearance of the temple was not the deepest reason for the abiding sense that its end would say something about the end of the world.

### The Temple in the Sacred Order
Second, the temple signified God's rule in the world. Jerusalem and its temple were the very center of Jewish thinking about the destiny of the world. This was the Holy City, described by teachers of Jesus' day as the point from which creation began. It was metaphorical to say, as they did, that Jerusalem was the highest place on earth. What this meant, of course, was that here heaven and earth found a place of contact. This was the dwelling place of the Lord God of Israel.

Therefore the very idea of Jerusalem and of the temple as "the dwelling place" of God conveys the Jewish belief in God's abiding presence in the world. It is the place where the order of heaven flows into the human order on earth. So long as Jerusalem's temple stands, God has his dwelling among human beings.

### The Temple in Sacred History
Third, the temple was a place of sacred memories. Its place is significant in the history of God's covenant with Israel. The temple mount is Mount Moriah, where Abraham brought Isaac for sacrifice (compare Gen 22 and 2 Chron 3:1). Abraham, father of the Israelite nation, said that this place would be called "The LORD Will Provide"—giving rise to the saying in Jerusalem, "On the mountain of the LORD it will be provided" (Gen 22:14).

It was here, in the fortress on Zion, that David set up his personal residence when he took Jerusalem from the Jebusites. He called the compound on Zion, where later he set up the tabernacle and made plans to build the temple, the City of David. It was here that God promised to establish the "house" (dynasty) of David, one that would "endure forever." The land on which the temple itself would be built was bought from a Jebusite for fifty pieces of silver, or about eighty dollars in today's money. There David built an altar and made a sacrifice that averted a devastating plague (see 2 Sam 24).

## The Temple in Sacred Space

Fourth, the temple was "sacred space." Solomon frankly admitted that the sanctuary on Mount Zion was a poor, small place—too small for a God whom "the heavens, even the highest heaven, cannot contain" (1 Kings 8:27). Yet he and his contemporaries thought of this place as a point of contact between the great God of heaven and earth and the one who seeks him. "May your eyes be open toward this temple night and day," Solomon prayed, "this place of which you said, 'My Name shall be there,' so that you will hear the prayer your servant prays toward this place" (1 Kings 8:29).

Even in antiquity, only the most literal-minded would think of God as actually housed in this structure, no matter how grand the scale. Nevertheless, all those who came to the temple would have surely been impressed with the utter separateness and distinctness of this place from the city at large, and indeed from every other place on earth. As building continued over the centuries, and especially after the rebuilding of the temple in 516 B.C.—the second temple dedicated almost precisely seventy years after the destruction of the first in 587/586— efforts were made to create a space isolated from the common sights and sounds of the community around.

The ministrations of the priesthood added to the aura of unworldly sanctity, giving weight to the impression that things done here were ordered and established from another world. In a remarkable letter from nearly two centuries before Christ, called the *Letter of Aristeas,* a Hellenistic Jewish writer described his admiration of the apparent spontaneity of priests who silently followed one movement after another in performing the sacrifices, all in concert, without spoken orders, effortlessly and apparently endlessly.

Of one priest he said, "We were greatly astonished when we saw Eleazar engaged in the ministration, at the mode of his work and the majesty of his appearance." Aristeas wrote of the priest's striking robe and the turban fastened by a golden tiara set with jewels on which the name of God was inscribed in sacred letters. Of this sight Aristeas said, "Their appearance created such awe and confusion of mind as to make one feel that one had come into the presence of a man who belonged to a different world."[3]

## The Temple as Re-presentation

Finally, this temple was strongly associated in antiquity with the world itself. It represented the cosmos: that is to say, it *re-presented* the world. I have already mentioned the fact that, for Israelites, here was a place where heaven and earth met and the concentric circles of divine potency flowed outward into the world, increasingly dissipated into the profane things of the world at large. In this regard, one would not be wrong to say that the thought associated with this temple was a common notion found among peoples and religious traditions around the world. Eric Voegelin, following others such as Mircea Eliade, has pointed out the determination of all peoples to locate symbols of divine involvement in the ambiguous hither and yon of the world and the helter-skelter of historical experience.

A temple, often established on a hill or a mountain, marked the place of a divine entry into the world. It is an *omphalos*—a "navel" or center of the world. In Europe I have seen many old maps of the "world" that depict Jerusalem as the very center of the earth's surface. This is a graphic way of expressing the idea that society continually strives to articulate or to "copy" a transcendent reality, one that is eternal and cannot be captured, only imitated on the level of profane earth and profane history.

The Jerusalem temple therefore depicted the things of the world while suggesting at the same time that their origin and source is from outside the world. The articles that made up the temple, the lamps, the incense, the bread, the "sea"—a vast above-ground pond of water—all suggested that which the world has or provides. So the temple was a small *cosmos;* only it was not the disordered cosmos that people experience around them, but a cosmos ordered from above. That is the difference. It was both an image of earth and an image of that which exists on a different level.

This twofold nature of Jerusalem and the temple, in the minds of pious Jews especially, came to light after the destruction of the earthly Jerusalem by the Romans in A.D. 70. More intensely than ever, Judaism—represented in apocalyptic writings like 2 Esdras and *2 Apocalypse of Baruch*—concentrated on the reality of a Jerusalem that is not touched by the flames of destruction and the murderous arrows of foreign armies. In 2 Esdras, Ezra's vision of a woman mourning the loss of a son ends with the woman being transformed into an "established city." The son represents the earthly Jerusalem that has been lost. But the vision of the city signifies the unshakable eternal city that is the true Jerusalem and the true place of sacrifice (2 Esdras 9:38—10:59).

Now we can begin to see how Jesus' disciples would have made the leap from "the destroyed temple" to a "destroyed earth." But we have not yet penetrated to the deepest level of their psychic and moral associations with this place. These associations came from centuries back, from prophetic forebodings about the destruction of the temple. They were feelings associated with the actual past—the Babylonian invasion in the sixth century B.C.—and the knowledge that God was capable of allowing such devastation to happen again.

## Why the Temple Must be Destroyed

Peter and the others could see the picture Jesus painted: the temple destroyed, the city in ruins, terror and suffering on every side, an endless tide of refugees with nowhere to flee. Babies starving, sick, crying; mothers in despair; unspeakable human misery. "How dreadful it will be in those days," said the Rabbi, "for pregnant women and nursing mothers. . . . For then there will be great distress, unequaled from the beginning of the world until now—and never to be equaled again" (Mt 24:19, 21).

Yet at the same time a thought would occur to Peter and each of the others. For the most part, it was a uniquely Jewish thought. Other peoples might attach some of the same significance to the fall of a temple and the destruction of a temple city as the Jews would: they would all see it as a cataclysmic rupture in the relationship between heaven and earth—between God and the human community. The Jewish companions of Jesus, however, would remember the prophets. More to the point, they would remember how the prophets had railed *against the temple*. They almost gave the impression at times that Israel would be better off without the monstrous, gaudy spectacle of feasts and sacrifices that distracted it from the real point of religion. "To obey is better than sacrifice," said Samuel, "and to heed is better than the fat of rams" (1 Sam 15:22).

And the great Isaiah—the oracle of Jerusalem itself and of Jerusalem's temple—his words they could not forget:

Hear the word of the LORD,
  you rulers of Sodom . . .
  you people of Gomorrah! . . .
Stop bringing meaningless offerings!
  Your incense is detestable to me.
New moons, Sabbaths and convocations—
  I cannot bear your evil assemblies. . . .
When you spread out your hands in prayer,
  I will hide my eyes from you. . . .
Your hands are full of blood;
  wash and make yourself clean. . . .
Stop doing wrong. (Is 1:10, 13-16)

The prophet Micah's sense of irony is stretched to the limit. How much can one sacrifice at the temple? he asks. And what good will it do?

Shall I offer my firstborn for my transgression,
    the fruit of my body for the sins of my soul? (Mic 6:7)

The one Jesus called Cephas, the "Stone"—the one we call Peter—could have recited that passage from Micah. He knew that it led up to the resonant lines contrasting with temple sacrifice three things that are most desired by the heart of God: "act justly . . . love mercy . . . walk humbly with your God" (Mic 6:8). It would be understandable if on this day he was thinking about these lines—words that pointed *beyond* the temple—with more than ordinary apprehension. It would have been a comfort to think of what lay beyond the temple, given the unsettling events of the days just past.

Perhaps Peter thought back to that day when he and the others drew near the city. Suddenly on approaching Jerusalem, Jesus grew pensive and quiet. His face was drawn and tight. Tears flowed freely when he caught sight of the distant city.

When he and the disciples entered the city, however, the mood changed to jubilation. The quiet rumors were now more boisterous and open; people were saying aloud, ever since they had left Jericho, what earlier had been said only secretly: "This Passover—the Messiah: here, at last, the Son of David!" A shout pulsated through the crowd, voices swelling in waves from the fortress Antonia to the district of Bethsaida. Again and again they shouted "Hosanna!" running, running, running toward the gleaming white rectangle that loomed above the balustrade on the hill. The circle of running, shouting people grew larger and larger around the figure on the colt as they pressed toward the temple.

What happened next, Peter thought, could not have been imagined either a day earlier or a day later. On that day, with the crowd singing his praises, the Rabbi struck the temple courts like lightning, scatter-

ing the merchants and moneychangers. Like distant thunder were his
words from the prophets Isaiah and Jeremiah: "My Father's house
shall be a house of prayer; you have made it a den of thieves" (Is 56:7;
Jer 7:8-11).

No one doubted the meaning of his words then. The temple must
not be profaned by the everyday pragmatic and financial interests of
this world—the interests of time—for the temple was a space given to
eternity. It was not the temple itself that gave offense to prophets, but
the inevitable vulgar association of the temple with things that pass
away with the flotsam and jetsam of time. The prophets had railed
against that real, earthbound, time-bound, vulgarizing temple so often
and so thoroughly that it seemed they might do away with the temple
itself and consider it no real loss. *That* the common people seldom
understood; but the aristocrats understood it too well, and were fear-
ful. On that day Jesus joined those voices, adding his own incompa-
rable pronouncement against the temple.

From that time on Peter may have detected a change in Jerusalem.
The crowds were still there. They followed Jesus willingly, hanging on
each word, arguing among themselves, gathering at the temple steps
to hear his teaching each morning. But in a subterranean fashion, the
mood had changed.

Peter did not know how he could tell. But he knew that the moment
of high expectation of a messianic coup of some kind had come and
gone. What was left, in the caves and recesses of Jerusalem's psyche,
on that Passover, was resentment. It was, in a sense, a resentment
against God. He had failed them again. He had not delivered them
from their circumstances. The people were making their decision, taking a new road—and rebellion was in their hearts.

### The Crisis

Do you know how sometimes while you are thinking about something,
a seemingly entirely unrelated image comes into your mind? Some

commonplace incident or some insignificant occurrence stored in the memory suddenly stirs the surface of the mind. Perhaps that happened to Peter, making him only vaguely aware of something immediately troubling. And even though it was troubling, he didn't know why. The flashing memory probably seemed innocuous enough. Perhaps he remembered how Judas let his purse fall heavily on the table while the Master spoke—and how he did so one more time when the Master used the expression (again) "Take up your cross."

We do not know, of course, how the disciples might have caught a sense of the crisis. We do know—and everyone really does have an intuition of this—that small things are connected with big things. And in this crisis we catch a glimpse of the seamless continuity between events in Jerusalem and a crisis facing the world itself. That is what the story of Christ's passion is all about.

Jesus was once again talking about suffering, not worldly triumph. He promised salvation to those who endured. He was always directing his disciples to the things that endured. And compared to that reality which lasts forever, even the temple showed the futility and the temporal nature of the world around. It only appeared to be permanent—it could not truly be. It only appeared to contain the angels and stars of paradise—in reality it opened itself daily to the profane, to erring human beings, to money tables and merchants with livestock to sell.

Jesus had captured their attention when he had said what must have seemed absurd. "You see all these, do you not?" Jesus made a sweeping gesture toward the megaliths lying about, the half-finished wall and the gilded capitals. "There will not be left here one stone upon another, that will not be thrown down."

What he said, and the peculiar intensity of his voice, put his disciples in a strangely reflective state of mind. Ever since they had started the journey toward Jerusalem, they had had a feeling that some cataclysm was in the making. In the run of events they sensed a strange combination of impending doom and glorious liberation. It was as if they had been hurled headlong into a story whose end they could not guess, but it impressed them as an adventure that, once begun, could not be averted. It was plotted out to the end; only their individual roles had yet to be decided.

The resoluteness with which Jesus, days earlier, had set himself on the road to Jerusalem had frightened his disciples, but it also enlarged their vision as never before. The Chinese term for crisis consists of two characters—one means danger and the other opportunity. That is a true depiction of crisis as we find it here. What would happen no one knew, but once the journey had begun they sensed that no one would come back unchanged; the wheat would be separated from the chaff. They might escape with only their lives—but life itself would be transformed. The fire would try them. Begin to release yourselves now from all that encumbers the journey, he urged them. "Sell your possessions and give to the poor. Provide purses for yourselves that will not wear out, a treasure in heaven that will not be exhausted, where no thief comes near and no moth destroys" (Lk 12:33).

When someone protested, "Lord, first let me go and bury my father," he said, "Let the dead bury their own dead, but you go and proclaim the kingdom of God" (Lk 9:59-60). And to another faint-hearted one, preoccupied with a passing world, he said, "No one who puts his hand to the plow and looks back is fit for service in the kingdom of God" (Lk 9:62). The persecution would come, but "do not be afraid of those who kill the body but cannot kill the soul. Rather, be afraid of the One who can destroy both soul and body in hell" (Mt 10:28). Then he repeated these words not once, but several times: "He who endures to the end will be saved."

The cords were severed, one by one. Souls became unanchored from the world of passing-away as they tethered themselves to the anchor of hope. Still, it was not easy to find the place where the anchor would hold. Most looked for another government, a new ruler. This is what *messiah* meant to most, even to Jesus' disciples. Power structures, misconstructed, had kept the misery so miserable and pressed down the oppressed. The new king would change that, and the kingdom of God would replace pagan kings, Idumean rulers and Roman emperors—or at least the Roman procurators.

It was the role of a prophet, however, that Jesus filled when he began to talk about the temple. The vision may have begun with this local concern, but the subject was altogether greater than the temple by itself. The temple provided a place for eyes to focus while Jesus painted a picture of the world being thrown down, stone by stone, until no one at all might be saved unless God shortened the days.

When the world is thus shaken, what will be left? That is the real question for a prophet. It is the one knowledge that life actually requires—the difference between what is lasting and what is not.

That is really the essence of a crisis. It takes the form of an ultimate decision; but it is also a decision close at hand. It faces specific, personal and realistic issues, but it actually forces a choice for or against that which is forever—that which is endlessly, eternally of value.

The variety of existence requires a greater variety of knowledge, but there is no higher knowledge. *Existence* requires that we know how to obtain food, how to prepare it, how to keep it and how to dispose of it. It requires that we know how to cooperate with others in order to build houses, dig wells and provide transportation; in order to hang a painting on the wall, attend a movie in the evening, fly to Los Angeles in the morning or read what happened in New York last night, we must understand the meaning of cooperation. It requires that we know how to educate our young so that they can collect all the bits and pieces of knowledge and acquire the skills needed for making a living, even if they fall far short of understanding life.

What *life* requires is infinitely less complex but painfully more difficult to come by. It requires that we make the finest of judgments, the subtlest distinctions. To know what lasts and what does not last requires not that we judge among things but that we draw a line

through the heart of everything separating flesh and spirit. It requires
an encompassing vision, one that sees the most massive and imposing
building as a heap of ruins, reduced by the ages. One that sees mountains worn to dust by the endless winds of change. One that sees in
everything its end. But it also requires a vision that sees through
impermanence and change to a lasting reality. The variety in time and
the variety in space speak not of themselves but of something beyond.
For one who can see, they provide the prism that reveals the shape
of hope.

But the world does not choose prophets or the prophetic vision
when it thinks it can cling to the familiar. To distinguish between what
lasts and what does not is to allow oneself to change. It is to endure
the pain of circumstances and be changed by them. Whenever possible, the world resists being changed; yet it very much desires a change
in circumstances. That crisis is very close to the crisis of time and
eternity—it is the comprehensive crisis, one that touches each of us,
all of us, and finally the world itself.

The temple stands ideally for that which lasts forever, while the
worshiper who goes there must seek to be transformed. Yet it also
participates in the changing world and can always be taken as a promise to change the world, as a favor to the worshiper who prefers it that
way. So when Jesus said that none of these things were really lasting,
the shock of disarray was intense for some.

The intent and the feeling were quite similar when Jesus said of his
body and blood, "This will be broken for you," and "This will be shed
for you." The Messiah seen and weak had to give way to the Messiah
unseen and mighty. Now the choice between time and eternity could
be made. It was the beginning of a crisis, but only the beginning. One
day it would be the world's crisis—and the world's last night.

Peter may haved remembered the purse slipping from the hand to
the floor, and the coins spilling out. They were quickly restored to
their place.

# 3

# The Way
# of the Kingdom

*Tell us . . . what will be the sign of your
coming and of the end of the age?*

*(MATTHEW 24:3)*

*T*HE WORD *COMING* IS OUR CLUE THAT THE UNDERLYING
subject is the kingdom of God. The Greek word is *parousia,* which
refers to the arrival of a king among subject peoples.

I want to underline the significance of this word—a word of anticipation—using a recent fishing story. This approach, by the way,
shouldn't be considered out of the ordinary. After all, the gospel itself,
we might say, begins with the best-known of all fishing stories (see Lk
5:1-11 for the full story, condensed in Mk 1:16-20 and Mt 4:18-22).
And this fish story, like that famous story, is a true one.

## A Fish Story
John, my ten-year-old son, and I went fishing one day at a large pond
in the country. We baited our hooks with chicken livers and dropped

our lines in the pond, fully expecting catfish to strike immediately at these gobby morsels we had dangled in the water.

Then we waited . . . and nothing happened. The murky brown-green water was opaque and placid, and seemed perfectly empty of fish. Aside from a few waterbugs and the chirping of late-afternoon frogs, we detected no signs of life. As the evening wore on, our hopes drooped.

On the other side of the pond, however, we noticed a man with tousled blond hair, wearing a worker's jeans and T-shirt, unloading his fishing gear. His quick, efficient movements told us immediately that this wasn't the first time he had fished in the pond. Soon he had two poles propped up on the bank with lines in the water.

Suddenly, a strike! Tossing his cigarette to the ground, he caught up his pole and began to reel in. The first catch was disappointing. It was a turtle. Pulling the creature to the bank, he wasted no time retrieving his hook. He threw the turtle back.

In a matter of minutes he had another strike, and he quickly reeled in a catfish—at least five pounds! In less than fifteen minutes he had another, and before a half hour had gone by he had two more. Deciding the action was too slow, he moved to a spot nearer to us.

Naturally, John and I longed to know his secret. At the same time something prevented us from approaching him immediately. Perhaps it was simply that he was a stranger; more probably it was his air of the serious fisherman who would perhaps be irritated at the questions of a couple of rank amateurs.

Soon John found his hook caught on the bottom of the pond. After a quick yank the line was out, but the hook, unfortunately, was gone. "That's our last hook!" John cried out.

Then the serious fisherman moved to my son's side, leaving his poles behind. He caught the end of John's line and looked at it briefly. "That didn't break," he said. "Your knot didn't hold." In a flash he pulled a number-2 hook out of his tackle box, along with two lead sinkers and a pair of pliers. With a few quick movements he had the new rig attached and ready to cast. "Let's find a forked stick," he said to John. And he showed him how to prop the whole affair up on the bank, tightening the line so as to reveal any tug from beneath the surface.

It seemed only moments before there was a sharp yank on the line. Now, time after time, John was pulling in catfish—losing some, throwing some back and keeping some.

All at once our perception of the water had changed. Rather than a still, muddy, lifeless pond, it was abundant with life. And just as suddenly the stranger had become an ally, a comrade in the cause of all fishermen.

What had he done? His experience and expertise were helps to us; but primarily he had changed our expectations, and thus our perception of reality. When we saw him reeling in fish, and even turtles, out of the pond, the pond no longer seemed so lifeless—and then when he came to my son's aid and guided him to the fish beneath that placid surface, John and I were finally able to see beyond that murky, quiet sheet of opaque water to the teeming life beneath. The expectancy of catching fish had altered and given power to our vision.

This principle operates in many realms of life. Expectancy is a part of perception. We remember our friends out of the happy thought of being together with them again. We see our enemies with the anxious thought of trouble ahead, with thoughts of retribution for past conflicts or with the dark thought of revenge. Our minds either embrace new challenges or recoil from them, based on what we have learned to expect. In the gestures of family members we see slights that others do not see at all. We notice the affectionate manner of one we love, while others see nothing beyond a pleasant smile. What we can see and know is in every way affected by what we anticipate.

Jesus did not "teach" about the kingdom of God the way a college professor teaches Greek history. Instead he caused his hearers to long for that kingdom and expect it. In doing so he disclosed to them the shape of a life and reality that heretofore they had never known to expect. This was not a theory or a kind of prognosis. It was the teaching of a *way,* a walk; it was the provision of an anticipatory life, one capable of proving the kingdom's reality.

This heightened sense of expectation has often been noticed in connection with Jesus' teachings on the kingdom. Albert Schweitzer, especially, saw the prominence of this tone of anticipation in the Gospel accounts. Few followed Schweitzer as far as he went in revising our picture of the life and teachings of Jesus. Nevertheless, his daring in taking into account the obvious apocalyptic nature of Jesus' teachings, and his questions about how the church adjusted to the loss of that sense of immediacy and the subsequent return to the tedium of everyday life, made an impact on a whole generation of biblical students.

Passed over too lightly, however, was the fact that this anticipation—this hope—is itself a way of knowing something, of learning or "seeing" something that is otherwise lost to us. This immediacy, this heightened anticipation, works to reveal the kingdom in a way that a mere prediction of the schedule of the kingdom never could.

### The Kingdom and Its Power
Why did Jesus' teachings raise such strong feelings of anticipation? How did he evoke the emotions and the aspirations that seemed to spread like wildfire around the nations of the Mediterranean in a matter of decades, uniting all varieties of ethnic groups in the first great international religion?

One might answer by considering four distinct levels of human awareness, each of which, in different ways, prompts the kinds of anticipatory feelings that change the way people "see" their world.

### Longing for the Kingdom
Let's begin with words from Scripture that people often take to imply the very opposite of "expectancy." They are often regarded (especially

by Transcendentalists and Hindus) as Jesus' endorsement of a spirit-ualized, inner, ideal reality: "The kingdom of God is within you" (Lk 17:21). It never seems to discourage these interpreters that nowhere else does Jesus appear to conform to their idea of a kind of Greek or Eastern mysticism.

Actually these words are loaded with a kind of moral paradox—one that, far from inviting inward contemplation, gives rise to an intense, outward-looking expectancy. We lose the strength of that paradox when we spiritualize the kingdom, making it a "private" reality.

For first-century Jews the expression *kingdom of God* was so strongly related to the community that no one would mistake it for a private or abstract reality unrelated to the community. It was truly a political concept. Often modern people, citing this fact, have in mind that the Jews were self-evidently mistaken. We think we know that the kingdom of God is a "spiritual" or a "future" reality, and that it therefore has nothing to do with present-day power struggles but ap-plies only to individuals. People of our generation, with our own cultural shortsightedness and our individualistic bias, forget that Jesus and his contemporaries were using terms that had strong ties to the nation of Israel.

When Jesus announced, and his Jewish auditors heard, the word *mal*$^c$*k̲û̲t̲*—"kingdom," as in kingdom of God—the idea of a new social and political reality was strongly communicated. The term meant, in a word, that God would be faithful to his promise. It expressed belief in a time when God's justice and not Roman "justice" would prevail—and when God's "way" would become manifest in the Jewish nation. It was a bedrock conviction that God would not *ultimately* allow his righteous ones to suffer. He would reward right and bring judgment against wrong.

These words, then, had the effect of evoking a *moral* expectancy. This is one of the most powerful emotions we know—the expectation of justice as an answer to wrong. On a very base level we know this feeling as the desire for revenge. A story that grips us and keeps us on the edge of our seats in a theater often begins with some atrocity, some great act of injustice that cries out for an answer. Black-hatted, uncouth outlaws lay waste a poor farmer's home, murder his children and leave his wife desolate with the house burning down and crops destroyed. The audience immediately begins to long for the farmer to find the culprits and exact a bloody justice. And we are not satisfied until the villains are overcome, the evil is requited, and we can *see* that justice has finally triumphed.

One of the reasons we enjoy a story of this kind is that we live in a world where this seldom happens. Even when justice formally wins out, it comes in a form that is far from perfect or satisfying. Further, there are no pure villains, and the justice and injustice that seem to struggle in the world of drama have only the most ambiguous and mixed representations in the real world.

Yet we still desire right and abhor wrong. And the prospect that our longing might be answered with real results is a powerful and attractive thought. It is true that we all tend to interpret the scenario of triumphant justice in a self-serving (and therefore inadvertently false) way. Nonetheless, we cannot deny also our love for the very idea of the triumph of right over wrong in the community of men and women. It is an enormously powerful, and often satisfying, emotion.

So Jesus was saying that this triumphant justice of the kingdom of God lies within the longing heart—the heart that yearns for justice or righteousness. Everywhere we turn in the Gospels we see Jesus recognizing the deep-seated desire within men and women for the right to prevail (or what we call "righteousness").

Just a few verses after Jesus' words "The kingdom of God is within you," we find parables reinforcing this great expectation. The first parable regards a women seeking justice from an unjust judge. After much persistence, she is finally given the justice she seeks. And Jesus follows this parable by saying:

Listen to what the unjust judge says. And will not God bring about justice for his chosen ones, who cry out to him day and night? Will he keep putting them off? I tell you, he will see that they get justice, and quickly. However, when the Son of Man comes, will he find faith on earth? (Lk 18:6-8)

This parable and the comments afterward have to do with justice in the community. The next parable, the parable of the Pharisee who is content with his self-righteousness and the tax collector who longs for mercy, has to do with a longing for one's own righteousness. Of course it is the tax collector who goes home "justified before God" (Lk 18:14). Again the kingdom is found in the anticipating and longing heart, not in the complacent present condition.

So this strength of a moral expectancy meets us at one level of Jesus' teachings. He touches a chord in our psychological makeup that is already highly charged—a desire to turn wrong into right and to see the right prevail.

## Watching for the Kingdom

The second level of Jesus' teachings, however, is more than a recognition of human desire. It is the assurance that outward conditions will satisfy the inward longing. More specifically, it is the assurance that *in the end* everything will yield to the righteous will of God in every way possible.

This means that people are invited to think about "the end" in very concrete and realistic ways. It was not an "opinion" or a prediction that would live among other such thoughts in the world of ideas. Instead it awakened a power that literally altered the pace and direction of history, because it made people think of their experience in terms of the "end" of things—which would spell the beginning of something much greater.

This new capacity to view the human experience through anticipation of the "last things," of an ultimate future, is traceable to a specific time in history. Mark records the time and the events:

After John was put in prison, Jesus went into Galilee, proclaiming the good news of God. "The time has come," he said. "The kingdom of God is near. Repent and believe the good news!" (Mk 1:14-15)

Since that time, wherever the gospel has had an influence, the tendency to understand ourselves as people expecting something, anticipating something—some new thing—has been noted. Even where Christianity is explicitly repudiated, the ingrained habit of seeing history as moving toward some immense new future has continued—and, in Marxism, has even been turned into a monstrous anti-Christian system. That is how powerful the Christian hope has become.

The utopian dream always included elements of the kingdom that Jesus caused people to anticipate. The peace, the community, the no-longer-alienated individual, the place where strangers were welcomed and prisoners were freed—these were all elements of the utopian dream.

For utopians and revolutionaries this dream would become reality as a result of human effort. It would be brought into reality by political force. It would be an artifact of human ingenuity and human compassion.

For hundreds of years this dream of peace, human freedom and finding a home in the world has held great power. From Christians like Thomas More to atheists like Karl Marx, the dream has doggedly followed the path of modern society, taking on forms both benign and monstrous. But the dream is there in the first place because Jesus taught his disciples to anticipate a reality of which these dreams are only distorted reflections.

The disciples learned to anticipate a real historical end and consummation. Therefore they began to see historical events in a new light. What was observed in history was understood to relate to God's historical purpose. People may not have understood how these things related to God's purpose—but *that* they were related became a confidence in what we call by names such as *providence* and *prevenient grace.*

The gospel was a way of anticipating intellectually, emotionally and socially—and therefore "seeing"—a reality that heretofore had been hidden. History had been like the eddies on the surface of a great lake, revealing only the superficial movements of temporal happenings. Now it had become a river, moving into the future and revealing at the same time the secrets beneath its clear, running water.

**Waiting for the Kingdom**
A third level of Jesus' teachings that evokes a strong expectancy has to do with the *coming* of the kingdom, or the second coming of the Lord himself. What we must notice about these teachings (and this is the reason I waited until now to mention them) is that they do not appeal to emotions of curiosity and fear; they do not invite specula-tion. Instead they have to do with the deep-seated ethical longing for justice or righteousness that I mentioned earlier. And what Jesus gives us is *an ethic of waiting* for his return.

The sayings that focus on the *coming* of the kingdom are in their most concentrated form in Matthew 24 and 25 and its parallels in the other Synoptic Gospels. These focus on the experience of waiting— waiting unaware of the judgment to come, as in the "days of Noah" (Mt 24:37-39); waiting like an owner of a house that anticipates a thief (24:43-44); waiting as faithful servants until the owner of the house returns (24:45-46); waiting not like a "wicked" servant who becomes greedy, slothful and cruel in the absence of the master (24:48-51); waiting like the bridal party, half of which is ready to wait all night if necessary and the other half of which is unprepared (25:1-13); and waiting like servants who invest their share of the master's resources wisely or unwisely while he is absent (25:14-30).

In each of these six parables—and in the seventh, which we shall come to shortly—we find the problems or possibilities that arise in the tension of waiting. Some of our most emotionally potent memories have to do with the experience of waiting. It is often the anticipation of something and not really the arrival of the moment itself that works most powerfully on our mental and emotional awareness of things— waiting for a wedding, waiting for the birth of a child, waiting for graduation, waiting for a promotion. Perhaps only with the exception of childbirth, the events we have anxiously awaited turn out to be anticlimactic. It is the anticipation that has engaged us at every level of awareness, preparing us for the fulfillment of the event itself, sometimes changing us within as the power of anticipation increases.

In these parables we find the illusion of normalcy in the present: Noah's age continued the routine of eating, drinking and marrying, never suspecting the future held untold disasters and judgment. We also find the wisdom of anticipating a future reckoning, the foolishness of cruelty or sloth in the light of that reckoning, and the purposefulness of using what we are given.

Let me note here that none of these invite *speculation* about the future. That is, they have little to do with a purely intellectual calculation about what is to come. Rather, these parables help us think about people in *relationship* to the future. Speculation actually avoids that kind of relationship—its purpose is to avert surprise or, in other words, to control the future from the present and thus not to be subject to the future. These parables, however, show men and women living to one degree or another subject to the future: ready for the future, preparing for the future, dreading the future or foolishly unaware of the time to come. They picture the meaning of our present in the light of a coming judgment, a reckoning, a reward or some drastic change. They disabuse us of the illusion of an unchanging present, and they set up the more realistic image of times, events, changes that are to come upon each of us.

Since they are not speculation, then, they are *moral* images of the future. That is, they have to do with the virtue of hope—a willing, trusting anticipation of what God will do. They emphasize the element of choosing how we meet the future—especially the ultimate future; the time of reckoning when the king, the master, the houseowner, the bridegroom will appear, a time when we will be called on to account for the time spent in anticipation of the day.

As you can see, this is quite different from speculation. For speculation gives us a certain kind of knowledge but requires nothing from us—it is, in fact, precisely the kind of knowledge that requires nothing in return. Personal knowledge is wisdom; it is the knowledge of what to do in the present. Hope, therefore, imparts a kind of wisdom. Speculation about the future is amoral—it purports to tell us everything, but actually fails to tell us the one thing we really need to know. By speculating we wish to navigate unharmed and unaffected and therefore unchanged through future circumstances; but moral anticipation changes *us*, because it requires that we act according to what we hope for and anticipate.

### Serving the King and Living in the Kingdom

Now we come to the highest level—a sort of capstone for the other levels, not only summarizing them but making them relevant to everything we do. At the first level we see that Jesus reminds his disciples of a deep-seated and until-now-unsatisfied longing for justice. At the second level, he assures them that finally (whenever "finally" will be) those longings will be satisfied. At the third level he speaks of the ethic of waiting—of living with a view of final judgment and final reward in mind.

This final level actually makes every passing moment transparent to the "last things" of world history. What does that mean? It means that at any moment we are making decisions, performing deeds, molding habits, building character that will be the ultimate meaning of our existence.

The six parables on the second coming that I have just briefly mentioned obviously come to some kind of a climax in the seventh parable, Matthew 25:31-46. Here we find the most beautiful and complete expression of that capstone level:

When the Son of Man comes in his glory, and all the angels with him, he will sit on his throne in heavenly glory. All the nations will be gathered before him, and he will separate the people one from another as a shepherd separates the sheep from the goats. He will put the sheep on his right and the goats on his left.

Then the King will say to those on his right, "Come, you who are blessed by my Father; take your inheritance, the kingdom prepared for you since the creation of the world. For I was hungry and you gave me something to eat, I was thirsty and you gave me something to drink, I was a stranger and you invited me in, I needed clothes and you clothed me, I was sick and you looked after me, I was in prison and you came to visit me."

Then the righteous will answer him, "Lord, when did we see you hungry and feed you, or thirsty and give you something to drink? When did we see you a stranger and invite you in, or needing clothes and clothe you? When did we see you sick or in prison and go to visit you?"

The King will reply, "I tell you the truth, whatever you did for one of the least of these brothers of mine, you did for me."

Then he will say to those on his left, "Depart from me, you who are cursed, into the eternal fire prepared for the devil and his angels. For I was hungry and you gave me nothing to eat, I was thirsty and you gave me nothing to drink, I was a stranger and you did not invite me in, I needed clothes and you did not clothe me, I was sick and in prison and you did not look after me."

They also will answer, "Lord, when did we see you hungry or thirsty or a stranger or needing clothes or sick or in prison, and did not help you?"

He will reply, "I tell you the truth, whatever you did not do for one of the least of these, you did not do for me."

Then they will go away to eternal punishment, but the righteous to eternal life.

In this parable it becomes clear that human hope is not just a matter of desiring justice where it cannot be found. Nor is Christian hope a matter of relegating those hopes confidently to a future fulfillment. Nor is it even a matter of transforming the time of waiting into a time of faithfulness and vigilance. All of these matters feed into a new kind of recognition.

It is the recognition that we do not choose the end *at the end,* but we choose our response to the end of things every day that we live. The King will one day come, and we have greeted his coming with honor, obedience and joy, or else we have said "Not now!" "Not here!" "Not with these people!" The King will one day judge, but in truth our actions of faith or unfaith, of love and mercy or contempt and hatred, are judged also at the moment we act.

This teaching of Jesus gives away the secret of the end of time. Speculation about the future has to do with a future that is still remote, and is kept remote by our attempt to understand it from afar. But this teaching reveals that the moment in which we live will be remembered at the end of time. It is a component of the end. And how we respond to this moment—this poor man in our midst, this starving child in our community, this prisoner in our institutions, the very humblest and meanest of those who enter our lives today—is in fact the way we greet the last moment of life, the last moment of the planet Earth, the first moment of a newly manifest and apparent kingdom of God.

You need not speculate vainly about the things that are to come. For the things to come—don't you remember?—have already happened to you. You need only remember them. In these are revealed with utter clarity the stream of history, and we know that the end of history can only be the disclosure of that within history which will last.

The rest will be consigned to destruction. And those who built their lives on it will hear the awful words "Depart from me . . ."

\*    \*    \*

"That being the case," you say, "then *when* these things happen shouldn't matter. And any question about 'when' is not at all relevant to Jesus' teaching. Is that what you're saying?"

Now, I'll admit that there is a certain convention in the interpretation of Jesus' teaching that wants to preserve credibility and integrity by not dealing with the question "When?" But that is not quite what I want to say here. I think it is legitimate, though risky, to ask the question "When?" So before you conclude that I have dodged that entire issue, I'd like to look at it in the next chapter.

# 4

# The Time
# of the Kingdom

*Tell us, when will these things happen?*
*(MARK 13:4)*

H OW LONG WILL THE PERFORMANCE LAST?" I ASKED A
friend who had already seen a play that my family and I had tickets
for.

"Too long!" he said. We were speaking on different sides of the time
question. If we are going to deal with the "time question" in Jesus'
teachings about the last things, then we need to understand a little
about both sides.

One side is really abstract. And that is what I was asking him: How
long, in terms of digital changes on a clock or the revolutions of the
works in my wristwatch, will the play last? How many hours and how
many minutes? Time considered that way has little to do with *what*
will happen. It has to do with a flat, featureless, uneventful duration.
It is a measure of time—time working or time playing ball, time on
a date or time waiting in a doctor's office. It makes no difference how

the time is spent or what event this time measures.

The Bible has little use for this abstract idea of time. This is particularly true of the Old Testament, which practically never speaks of duration of time except in reference to the specific content and meaning of that time. It speaks, for instance, of the "days of Solomon." In the New Testament, the writers could have used the Greek term *chronos,* which meant a duration or measure of time. But they seldom used it. Luke, the most Greek-oriented of the writers, is the one who used it most.

The other side of the time question is represented in the Greek word *kairos,* a term denoting a particular kind or quality of time. It is what my friend had in mind when he said, "Too long!" To say the play lasted an hour and forty-five minutes did not describe *his* experience of the play. And I think one could make the argument that even today this quality of time is what we think of first and most often, though we *communicate* with others in terms of "an hour and forty-five minutes." We think of a "happy time," "a tedious and boring time," "a time when opportunity knocked." The time we spent was sad, adventurous, joyful, "a learning experience." It was childhood "days of wonder," a midlife "crisis" or the "golden years." We don't usually say things happened "over a nine-month period"; we're more likely to say "when we were expecting Emily." It's not "in 1966" that things happened nearly so often as it's "when I was in college."

We fill time with content. We give it feeling and color, purpose and pace. This is ninety percent of the way we think about time. Ancient people were just forthright enough to say so and didn't fall back on abstractions as much as we do. That's an important difference. And it is naturally this sense of time we find far more frequently in the Bible.

## Jesus' Response to the When Question
Now we are ready to take note of something rather remarkable and important.

Even though first-century Jews would not have been as occupied with the issue of the kingdom's appearance on a time line as we are today, they were in fact quite interested in God's power and inclination to change the *character* of the times. The change they asked about was not just a change in *chronos,* but a change in *kairos.* Whether the kingdom of God might have been considered present, in the imminent future or in an undetermined future was not as important as the conviction that the Jews' waiting would not go unrewarded. God would change things. Injustice would be answered by God's justice. Faith would be answered by God's faithfulness. The temporary hiddenness of God's purposes would at some time be replaced by the *epiphany*— God's own disclosure of his sovereign rule among the nations, God's kingdom.

Does this expression of qualitative change evade the question of when? Not at all. It only puts the matter in a different light. We do, after all, ask, "When will this play come to an end—or get better?" or "When will this baby arrive?" or "When will this person grow up?" In view of the expectations Jesus taught his disciples, the most natural question to ask is "When will these things happen?" (Mk 13:4). "When?" means, in this case, "Under what circumstances? What will be the indications that the time has arrived? What are the signs?"

Not only do Jesus' contemporary listeners seem to be interested in this question of when, but the way Jesus answers them can now be understood as precisely to the point. Jesus himself never takes exception to the questions they ask, and if they are dissatisfied with his answer, the Gospels certainly never tell us so. Other than to caution his listeners that "no one knows about that day or hour" (Mt 24:36), he never casts doubt on the appropriateness of the question. (That in itself is very unlike modern attitudes that would squelch anything that smells of the apocalyptic!) While they may not know about the "day or hour," there are things they ought to know that are quite important in answering that very question. And he proceeds to say what those things are.

Now, before we take note of what the Gospels specifically report about the responses to these questions, let's look at a common objection. "This is not an answer; it's an evasion" might be one response. Jesus seems to communicate to his disciples a clear sense of urgency and expectancy. But now we might ask, did the Gospel writers smooth the sharp edges of his apocalyptic announcements because they no longer expected the imminent parousia?

We need not deny that the Evangelists had a concern for this very matter. We can see it playing a large part in Luke-Acts. When the resurrected Lord is asked if at this time he will establish the kingdom, his reply becomes in effect the theme of Acts. This is not for Jesus' disciples to know, we are told; but they are to take the gospel to Judea, Samaria and the uttermost parts of the world (Acts 1:7-8). The time before the parousia is the time God is actively redeeming the world through the gospel of grace. We are living in salvation history—the time of redemption, between the "already" of Christ's coming in humility and the "not yet" of his coming in glory. That vision of history certainly emerged from the critical question of what history "after Jesus" means.

But what about the immediate concerns of Jesus and his disciples in their own day? Volumes have been written on the difficulty of getting back to that precise picture, because the Gospels naturally have given us a picture of those days in light of (1) the crucifixion of the Lord, (2) the subsequent days of desperation and fear, (3) the glory of the resurrection and (4) the progress of the gospel in the power of the Holy Spirit.

But the question whether Jesus or the Gospel writers evaded the self-evident question "When?" can be answered satisfactorily, I think, when we give attention to the pattern of the responses we find in the Gospels. Because what we do find in the Gospel accounts is an undeniable conviction and coherence in the many sayings in reply to the question "When?" And only after we detect the nature of these answers can we judge whether Jesus' response was an invitation to speculate about the time of the end, a clever evasion of the question or something entirely different and perhaps more direct than we might guess at first glance.

In fact, what we find on close inspection lacks all the smoothness of a clever evasion. The gospel teaching on the end of time is a huge rock heaved into the middle of our quiet pond of theological systems and devotional Christianity, upsetting everything. Speculation becomes impossible, but anticipation is set on "high." This disturbance comes to light in four main points.

*1. No one knows the day, not even Jesus himself.* Matthew and Mark read, "No one knows about that day or hour, not even the angels in heaven, nor the Son, but only the Father" (Mt 24:36; Mk 13:32). The same point is recalled by Luke in a saying of the resurrected Lord. In Acts he is asked, "Lord, are you at this time going to restore the kingdom to Israel?" Jesus answers, "It is not for you to know the times and dates the Father has set by his own authority" (Acts 1:6-7).

These statements refute any attempt to place the parousia of Christ and the end of the age on the calendar. The many attempts to do so have inevitably come to grief. But it's important in light of that to grasp the sense in which the question "When?" might be answered *other than in a chronological sense.*

My son might well ask me, "When can I watch television?" And I could answer in a perfectly straightforward way by saying, "You can watch television when you finish your homework." That answer satisfies the question of when by referring to a condition rather than to a time on the clock. Or he may ask, "When can I go out and play?" And his mother may answer, "When it stops raining." Thus she might refer to conditions over which he has no control, and still make no promise with regard to chronological time.

What we have in these sayings of Jesus in reference to time is not an evasion but a clear and direct answer. The "when" of the kingdom's disclosure cannot be answered with a mere reference to the abstraction of chronological time.

2. *When the kingdom is revealed it will be apparent to everyone, everywhere, at once.* Jesus used an Aramaic idiom when he said, "Where there is a dead body, there the vultures will gather" (Lk 17:37; compare Mt 24:28). This saying implies something that I want to return to later; but at one level at least it suggests the openness of the events of the last days. Everyone for miles around can see vultures circling in the air—thus Jesus shows that he is speaking of an event that will be visible and public, not hidden from the view of all but the initiated. Such will be the coming of the kingdom in glory.

The other saying that expresses the same reality is "For the Son of Man in his day will be like the lightning, which flashes and lights up the sky from one end to the other" (Lk 17:24; compare Mt 24:27). Nothing could be clearer: *when* the kingdom appears, it will not be a matter of privileged information; everyone will know. "So if anyone tells you, 'There he is, out in the desert,' do not go out; or 'Here he is, in the inner rooms,' do not believe it" (Mt 24:26).

3. *When the kingdom comes, it will come in the course of ordinary life.* There will not be the gradual, stage-by-stage overtaking of the kingdom time but a sudden break into the ordinary affairs of life. To make this point, Jesus recalls two instances of judgment from Genesis: Noah's flood and the story of Sodom's destruction. The point is not, as some have taken it to be, the unusual bustling about of those days; it is the apparently common and ordinary course of events—"eating, drinking, marrying, and being given in marriage, . . . buying and selling, planting and building" (Lk 17:27-28).

The kingdom's coming will be an abrupt break into time. It will take most people by surprise. They will expect only the next day, and they will discover the last day.

These three points in answer to the question "When?" are the setting for the central teaching of Jesus about the coming of the kingdom. The *time* question will not yield to our ordinary reading of the signs, nor to our calculation of dates and seasons. Nevertheless, there is a point in talking about the time. For the time of the end, the time of the glorious revealing of the kingdom, is a matter of the heart's disposition. It is an orientation of the life toward that glorious manifestation of God's work. It is a time one must carry about in the ordinary affairs of life. It is "within you," or "among you" (Lk 17:21). It is that for which you must *watch* and *be ready*. "Therefore keep watch, because you do not know on what day your Lord will come" (Mt 24:42).

However, precisely because it comes without warning in the midst of everyday living, it also becomes relevant to ordinary daily life. Since we do not know when we will see Christ coming, we must all the more be ready at any time. Thus *every* day, not just the last day, comes under the scrutiny of this question: "When the Son of Man comes, will he find faith on the earth?" (Lk 18:8). Each day, with its crises and decisions, its opportunities to witness to the truth or to evade the truth, becomes a living answer to God as he offers the kingdom. Each day is a choosing of life or a choosing of death.

If the parousia, or the return of Christ in glory, were only the last thing on the historical agenda, then it would be meaningful as the last act in world history, but less so as we imagine the eschaton receding into the remote future. The more remote, the less relevant. But as long as the time is indeterminate—as long as "no one knows about that day or hour . . . but only the Father"—the end of history becomes equally important for every day in history. The end of history is not the culmination of a process but the judgment of every day and every action.

### The Times, the Seasons and the Judgment of God
Assuming that these first three points were *all* that Jesus said about

the *time* of the kingdom's coming, I can well imagine someone saying that time is irrelevant to the question of his coming. If He should come at just any time, in response to nothing but God's very arbitrary time-table—an abstract end time that is known to God but to no one else—why would he ever have raised the question among his disciples? Why would he have entertained their questions?

But there is one more item to take into consideration here. So far we have seen that (1) the specific time is unpredictable, (2) but when it comes it will be apparent to all and (3) it will break into the routine of ordinary life. All of these points have a bearing on the conviction that God will respond to our times and that "that day" cannot be understood simply as God's response to a timetable. Yet the last major point that should be made about Jesus' answer to the question of when is perhaps the most important one.

*4. When the kingdom comes, it comes in judgment of a world in sin and rebellion against God and with the sure prospect of deliverance from evil for those who have acknowledged the kingship of Christ.* Both the judgment of God and the good news of a Savior will be made known. The entire world will be confronted with the utter futility of evil and the rightness of obedience to God's will. God will not be responding to a timetable, then, but he will be responding to the need for judgment—for setting things right. So the coming of God's king-dom is no abstraction but a concrete, visible, inevitable response to evil and to the hope for righteousness. The "when" question therefore refers to concrete *conditions,* not to an abstract point in chronological time.

You will know the answer to the question "When?" Jesus said, because "where there is a dead body, there the vultures will gather" (Lk 17:37; compare Mt 24:28). Here is a secular idiomatic expression that refers first to something that is open and public and cannot be hidden. But it also carries the connotation of offense, of corruption and death. These things draw the vultures, just as evil draws the judgment of God. The image is not a pretty one. It was not intended to be.

Taking Matthew 24 as a point of reference, we find that in verses 4-9 Jesus reiterates for the disciples what can be expected in any time: false Christs and deceptions (vv. 4-5), wars and rumors of wars, famines, earthquakes and persecutions (vv. 6-9). And he also refers to matters that come with particular intensity and with an air of imminent crisis:

At that time [not just *any* time] many will turn away from the faith and will betray and hate each other, and many false prophets will appear and deceive many people. Because of the increase of wickedness, the love of most will grow cold, but he who stands firm to the end will be saved. (vv. 10-13)

The moment we attempt a time line with this vision, things begin to break down. Telescoped into this prophetic oracle of Jesus are the horrors and temptations and degradations of a world caught in the destructive forces of its own sin. In one way these things have always occurred since the day he spoke the words. In another way there have been critical times when the words were especially applicable. And in yet another way, they are the character of the times as we approach the end.

All of these things are true. But this teaching highlights the fact that what God will do at the end of time is a response not merely to a timetable but to the condition of human life. Therefore, the one sure answer we have about the end of time and the coming of God's kingdom is that it will be in response to the need for *judgment* and *deliverance*.

The time is unpredictable and indeterminate in the abstract—but in the concrete (namely, in terms of the state of the human condition) it is quite predictable. That is, we can be sure that when human beings sin, God will come in judgment. We can be sure that God has never lost interest in the human predicament, even down to the end of time.

So when we see these things happening—wickedness, godlessness, lovelessness, persecution and violence—we can be just as sure that the kingdom of God approaches.

Drawing the connection between a world in chaos and suffering and the approaching kingdom, Jesus told a parable:

Look at the fig tree and all the trees. When they sprout leaves, you can see for yourselves that summer is near. Even so, when you see these things happening, you know that the kingdom of God is near. (Lk 21:29-31; also see Mt 24:32-33; Mk 13:28-29)

This was important also to Paul's teachings on the last things. God's judgment of evil and his deliverance of his people from evil are certain, Paul pointed out to the anxious end-time speculators of Thessalonica. Concerning "times and dates," he said, "you know very well that the day of the Lord will come like a thief in the night" (1 Thess 5:2). But since each one knows what God requires—self-control, faith, love and hope in face of the suffering of this life (v. 8)—"you brothers are not in darkness so that this day should surprise you like a thief" (v. 4). You will not be taken by surprise, Paul insists, not because you know ahead of time when it will happen, but for the very reason that you know the nature of evil and are alert to God's sure response against evil and for the deliverance of his saints.

"We belong to the day," Paul said. Only those who are asleep in sin will be surprised—because God's response to the condition of evil is sure.

### The Presence of the Kingdom

Knowing the good news of God's sure response to evil and his promise to deliver those who belong to him helps us understand why Jesus often taught about the kingdom as a present reality.

I live a few miles inland from the Atlantic Ocean. At times I will go for weeks without even seeing the ocean, but I'm often reminded of its presence in other ways.

This morning as I drove to town I could see a line of cumulus clouds stretching the length of the eastern horizon. There was a bright, luminous, blue-green cast to those clouds that gave off an almost neon effect in broad daylight. The clouds were catching rays reflected from the ocean's surface.

In a similar way, the realization that God responds to evil and contends for righteousness casts a bright light onto the foreground of every moment in history. Each day we are met with choices. In each choice we are called upon to acknowledge the sovereignty of God. For those who "watch" as Jesus enjoined, that last great reality of the kingdom of God is with them in every decision; it is a constant orientation of life.

Does it have to do with the future? Yes, with the future of all things, all peoples, all actions; each daily reality finds its goal and meaning in the end of all things in God's sovereign rule. Does it have to do with the present? Is it a "realized" kingdom? Yes it is, in that choices pertaining to the goal of life are with us each day and each moment. Ask not, "What day?" and "What season?" for in *this* day we choose the end. In *this* day we choose how we are to meet God on the great day of judgment.

Now, it is this connection with judgment that finally allows us to talk about the "time" of the kingdom and the "time" of the end in the way Jesus related it to his disciples. You know from the earlier chapters how reluctant I have been to approach this question of the time. And yet we also see now how natural and how inevitable the question is, and we note that the Gospels betray no hint of censure of those who ask the question. (We moderns have been most critical, revealing our prejudice against the very notion of raising such a natural and inevitable point!) But now, with a bit of effort to overcome another modern prejudice—the prejudice against the idea of divine judgment—we can begin to catch a glimpse of that one central point Jesus makes about the historic conditions that mark the end of time.

# 5

# The Coming Judgment

*How dreadful it will be in those days. . . .*
*Pray that this will not take place in winter,*
*because those will be days of distress*
*unequaled from the beginning, when God*
*created the world, until now—and never*
*to be equaled again. If the Lord had not cut*
*short those days, no one would survive.*

*(MARK 13:17-20)*

*Take the talent from him and . . . throw*
*that worthless servant outside,*
*into the darkness, where there will be*
*weeping and gnashing of teeth.*

*(MATTHEW 25:28, 30)*

*N*O DOUBT JESUS' VIVID DEPICTION OF THE WRATH OF GOD
is troubling to many modern readers. This is because we have lost the
connection between God's mercy and God's wrath, and we think we
can have the former without the latter. And it is all the more troubling
to us because references to divine judgment seem intertwined with all
of the teachings on eschatology. This is a good point at which to stop
and consider the meaning and the importance of these references to
God's judgment in the Gospels, and especially in Matthew 24—25,
along with the parallels in Mark and Luke.

Jesus minced no words. No less, certainly, than those of an Old
Testament prophet, his words rang with the urgency of warning. He
foretold national and social disaster (Mt 24:6-8), persecutions (vv. 9-
11) and the temptation to lose heart and fall away from the faith

because of general disorder and tribulation (vv. 12-13).

It is true that many of these disasters and warnings had to do with local events in Judea. We have already noted how important was the fact that this teaching began in a prediction of the temple's destruction, which then occurred in A.D. 70. In Luke 21:20 Jesus also refers to a siege of Jerusalem by surrounding armies. These were clearly local Judean events, and Jesus' words can refer to those events that are now long past. But since we know that New Testament writers considered prophecy as something that could be fulfilled in more than one way and at more than one time, we should not assume that these words are fully exhausted by the events of A.D. 70.

Aside from these references to Jerusalem and Judea, the text leads us to envision a much more comprehensive disaster, one of global—if not universal—proportions:

Immediately after the distress of those days

"the sun will be darkened,

and the moon will not give its light;

the stars will fall from the sky,

and the heavenly bodies will be shaken." (Mt 24:29)

On the earth, nations will be in anguish and perplexity at the roaring and tossing of the sea. Men will faint from terror, apprehensive of what is coming on the world. (Lk 21:25-26)

All of these events, whether in Jerusalem or in a much broader arena of activity, are seen as results of wrath and of judgment. Concerning Jerusalem, Jesus specifically uses the word *wrath (orgē):* "There will be great distress in the land and *wrath* against this people" (Lk 21:23). At the coming of the Son of Man, he notes, the "nations of the earth will mourn" (Mt 24:30).

In Matthew's rendering of the Mount of Olives teaching, chapters 24 and 25 end with a series of seven parables, of which four refer explicitly to the punishment of the wicked. First we see Jesus reminding his disciples of the wrath against the world in the days of Noah

(24:39). Next a parable depicts an unfaithful servant discovered by his returning master, who "will cut him to pieces and assign him a place with the hypocrites, where there will be weeping and gnashing of teeth" (24:51). Skipping over the "foolish virgins" who are merely shut out of the wedding reception (not my idea of a punishment anyway), we see what happens to the "worthless servant" who had buried his one talent out of fear of his master: he is thrown "outside, into the darkness, where there will be weeping and gnashing of teeth" (25:30). And finally, in the parable of the dividing of the people, which is like the dividing of sheep and goats, the goat-people are condemned by the judge-king: "Depart from me, you who are cursed, into the eternal fire prepared for the devil and his angels" (25:41).

These are harsh words. If "gentle Jesus, meek and mild" describes one's image of the Lord, then these sayings are bound to produce a rude shock. It is necessary, in our day, to rediscover why the God of mercy who came as "infant holy, infant lowly"[1] is not altogether incompatible with the Lord of hosts whose coming is also an occasion for anguish, since

Every eye shall now behold him,
robed in dreadful majesty;
those who set at naught and sold him,
pierced and nailed him to the tree.[2]

It was the Jewish scholar Abraham Heschel who, in my own experience, best expressed the ultimate compatibility of these two images. In his famous work *The Prophets* he sets in relief the great distinctiveness of the Hebrew prophets' understanding of God as a God of pathos. It is best to see this idea in contrast to the philosophy of Aristotle. Aristotle, somewhat like the Hebrews, believed in one God. He assumed, however, that oneness implied that God is complete within himself and lacking nothing. Since suffering comes from love or desire for something, God cannot suffer. Aristotle's God, unlike human beings, does not suffer. He is *a-pathetic*. He does not exhibit passions like "desire, anger, fear, confidence, envy, joy, friendly feeling, hatred, longing, jealously, pity" or experience those states of consciousness that are accompanied by pleasure or pain.[3]

In the experience of the biblical prophet, by remarkable contrast, God is "moved and affected by what happens in the world, and reacts accordingly." The God of the Bible is far from being detached and unaffected, "apathetic," as Aristotle would have it. "In the biblical view, man's deeds may move Him, affect Him, grieve Him or, on the other hand, gladden and please Him. This notion that God can be intimately affected, that He possesses not merely intelligence and will, but also pathos, basically defines the prophetic consciousness of God."[4]

Heschel saw that for the prophets, pathos does not imply an anthropomorphic vision of God (a view of God "in the form of a human being"). But what it does clearly imply is that God chooses to live in *relationship* to that which he has created. Pathos implies not physical suffering but the intervention of a relationship.

We can all believe that a mother suffers because of a sick child. She does not suffer physically, but she enters into the suffering of the child. In her suffering she is *sym-pathetic*—as opposed to Aristotle's lone god, who is apathetic. She suffers with her child. The God known by the prophets was a God sympathetically suffering with his people.

Therefore God reacts to his people. He responds to them, and they experience this as "the pathos of love or the pathos of anger."[5]

### "I Have a Problem with God's Anger"

The problem that predictably intrudes on this understanding of God came to light one day in a systematic theology class when Kevin said, "I have a problem with this idea of God's anger."

"What is the problem?" asked another student, who had become convinced by Heschel's work and had also read Dale Moody, a Christian theologian who reflected similar thinking.

"Well," Kevin replied, "when I think of anger, I think of someone who is out of control. That's not what I would want to believe about God; it would make life too uncertain."

Kevin had put his finger on a common objection to the idea of a God of pathos. And most of us have absorbed (even unconsciously) enough Aristotelian ethics to believe that emotions that teeter-totter too far in one direction or another upset the apple cart of civility.

This misunderstanding of God's love, or God's anger, does come from an anthropomorphic misreading of the prophets. "God's pathos," wrote Heschel, "was not thought of as a sort of fever of the mind which, disregarding the standards of justice, culminates in irrational and irresponsible action." Since the Bible consistently presses the view that "there is justice in all His ways," then the conclusion must be that

there is no dichotomy of pathos and ethos, of motive and norm. They do not exist side by side, opposing each other; they involve and presuppose each other. It is because God is the source of justice that His pathos is ethical; and it is because God is absolutely personal—devoid of anything impersonal—that this ethos is full of pathos.[6]

In the history of Christian doctrine, as Heschel points out, the person whose opposition to the anger of God created the greatest waves was Marcion, the Gnostic heretic of the second century. Marcion insisted on God's dispassionate nature. This God of anger and wrath that the Hebrew prophets spoke of, therefore, must be very different from the God whom Jesus had come to reveal. The Jewish God was "judicial, harsh, mighty in war . . . the author of evils . . . ignorant, cruel, inconsistent, inscrutable, and wicked." But the God of Jesus was "mild, placid, and simply good and excellent."[7] Even the church father Tertullian, the uncompromising foe of the Marcionite heresy, wanted to disavow passions for God the Father and attribute them only to God the Son. Thus Tertullian found himself projecting a dualistic theology of "the impassible Father and the irascible Son."[8]

   Discussion within the church over this issue was quite extensive and not a little complicated. It is enough to point out here that our modern desire to reject the idea of God's wrath has a long and venerable tradition. Many have understandably feared that a Hebrew *anthropopathy* (attribution of human suffering to God) was not far removed from the pride, boasting, envy and lusts attributed to the Greek deities. But others, like the early Christian apologist Lactantius (c. 240-320), understood that God could not very well love us if he did not hate the sin that brought us to harm and death. And in the age of the Reformation, Luther "used to boast that he had spoken more strongly of the divine wrath than had been done" under Catholicism.[9]

### The Comfort of Wrath

In *Night,* Elie Wiesel's memoir of a Nazi concentration camp during World War II, he tells of three prisoners condemned to be hanged. Two men were accused of hoarding arms. The third, a young boy much loved in the camp, had refused to give information under torture. The three were made to stand on chairs, ropes around their necks; the one in the middle was the young boy, light of body and frightened. Inmates were lined up in ranks, forced to watch.

   The chairs were kicked out from under the victims. The two adults died quickly, but not the boy. He writhed in anguish, suffocating slowly.

   Someone muttered, "Where is God?" And no one answered. Later, as the prisoners were being led away from the place of execution, the question was asked again: "Where is God now?"

   Wiesel heard the answer within him: "Where is He? Here He is— He is hanging here on this gallows."[10]

   God comforts his people because he is intimately acquainted with their suffering and affliction. This intimacy of God in the suffering of this world is an essential element in the Hebrew prophetic theology.

Does this experience of God apply also to sin? Does it pertain not only to our innocent bearing up under temptation and persecution but also to the tendency we have to harm ourselves? If the answer is yes, would we not then experience God's comfort or concern as the sting of wrath? We have taken the wrong road, and God wishes to set us right. And in doing so his actions may deal a drastic blow to our plans, our purposes and what we had formerly experienced as a joyride (downhill).

What Heschel and others have identified as the Hebrew experience of God implies that God must be known—and can only be known—in terms of an interaction with his people. His eye is upon us; he is ever attending to our needs, our progress, our aspirations, our failures, our ignominious rebellion. He is willing to forgive everything, but he will overlook nothing. He is closer than a brother. He is our next of kin. We experience that intimacy as love, the strength of his companionship, but also as correction, as guidance and, if we persist, as wrath.

Humans are never "on their own," as the Marxist writer Ernst Bloch said. Instead we are always in relationship. *Wrath* refers to one side of that relationship. It is an experience of God's love for his creation. When we stubbornly refuse that love out of rebellion and disobedience, we experience, by our own actions, the loss of that love. So we sometimes experience the passionate love of God as wrath. God will not hold us in relationship. That is not the way of love. But if we fail to experience any love or any rescue from calamity when we rebel, that should not be interpreted as love. It should be seen as indifference.

Jonathan Edwards's sermon "Sinners in the Hands of an Angry God" used to appear in many high-school textbooks as an example of early American literature. The effect was generally, "What frightful ideas those old Puritans had about God!" And, in truth, I'm not at all sure Edwards's approach would find a responsive audience today, even among evangelical Christians who might be expected to be sym-pathetic to the general theme. But it occurs to me that there is a contrast to this image of Edwards's sermon that is even more unnerving, in any age. The contrasting sermon title might be "Mortals in the Hands of an Indifferent God."

The chord of reality struck by the prophets of the Bible is our insatiable need for a life that does, after all, matter to someone. "Wrath" we can face if we must. And if it embodies a norm that says to us, "Yes, what you do really matters, and it really does have consequences—both now and forever," then we are at least encouraged that we are not shouting into a void or living in a free-fall into a valueless abyss. What we cannot endure is indifference, a life that really doesn't matter to anyone because the God of this life is somehow apathetic.

### The End of Evil, the Endless Mercy

Judgment in the prophetic oracles and in the teachings of Jesus is not seen in arbitrary outbreaks of divine anger that have no purpose. This is an essential point. The wrath of God that comes in such great doses in, for instance, Matthew 24—25, focuses on "the end." Jesus said, in the face of these troubles to come, that "he who stands firm to *the end* will be saved" (24:13). Further, "this gospel of the kingdom will be preached in the whole world as a testimony to all nations, and then *the end* will come" (v. 14).

Now, what this *end* refers to may at first glance be uncertain. "The end of what?" we must ask. Naturally, those whose interpretation of eschatology expects a millennial kingdom to follow—the one mentioned in Revelation 20—would not see this "end" as the end of history. Other interpretations, amillennial and postmillennial, would perhaps call it the end of history, but not the end of our experience with God. All Christian eschatologies anticipate a new heaven and a new earth. So in what sense can Jesus be referring to the end?

Clearly, the focus in these teachings is on *the end of evil.* Therefore judgment portends that end and testifies to the belief that those things which oppose God, defile the world and undermine humanity—the agents of war, disease, crime, revenge, hatred, envy and lust—will come to an end. Judgment, in its many forms, is about that end.

The gospel is the assurance that those things that *should* last *will* last. Those things that keep people in community, that express the love of God for his creation, will never be lost, whereas that which destroys, maims and invalidates life will finally be overcome. That which God has intended from the beginning will never end: "Heaven and earth will pass away, but my words will never pass away" (Mt 24:35; Mk 13:31; Lk 21:33). The "word" is that which God has willed from the beginning. It is this word that Jesus proclaims. And the gospel is that the Word that "was with God" and "was God" and in whom "was life" shall not be overcome (Jn 1:1-5).

To believe that judgment properly has its place in Christian eschatology is to believe that good will ultimately prevail and that evil will finally be overcome. For only judgment speaks of the incompatibility between the world God created in love and the hatred of that world. Without judgment God's love fades into indifference.

# 6

# The False
# Messiah

*Watch out that no one deceives you.*
*Many will come in my name, claiming,*
*"I am he," and will deceive many. . . .*
*At that time if anyone says to you,*
*"Look, here is the Christ!" or, "Look,*
*there he is!" do not believe it. For false Christs*
*and false prophets will appear and perform*
*signs and miracles to deceive the elect—*
*if that were possible. So be on your guard;*
*I have told you everything ahead of time.*

**(MARK 13:5-6, 21-23)**

*I*N 1993 A BLAZING HOLOCAUST ON THE TEXAS PLAINS MARKED the end of yet another "messiah." David Koresh was not the first, nor will he be the last.

In times of growing social stress it seems that messianic figures spring up with the regularity of mushrooms. Some are eccentrics, never likely to have broad influence, yet sometimes they become tragically authentic pied pipers leading the innocent or deluded to destruction. A good historian could easily list a dozen since the days of Konrad Schmid of Thuringia, the David Koresh of the fourteenth century.

But what truly makes the twentieth century remarkable in this regard is not the occasional turning up of a local fanatic with his stash of AK-47s and a vision from God, or the even more appalling turnout of willing followers, sometimes numbering in the hundreds. Nor is it even the storm and stress of our times that seem to make these events plausible. It is a certain subtle messianic predisposition.

The phenomenon that proves this predisposition is the widespread outbreak *and growth* of messianic-type movements. Once such movements would have been confined to the scale of Koresh's little group, but some have recently grown into great mass movements capturing whole nations, moving out into the world as historic forces. Most of twentieth-century history can be written as a story of how the world has responded to one messiah after another—or, if not to a messiah, at least to some promise of deliverance on an apocalyptic scale. People of the twentieth century, like never before, have learned to expect a new world regularly. Almost every decade in the first half-century brought a new messiah: Lenin, then Mussolini, then Stalin, Hitler, Mao. Throughout the century we have been preoccupied, in one way or another, by communism, fascism, Nazism and the social chaos left in the wake of these messianic movements.

What is difficult to fully appreciate, since we are so close to our times, is the degree to which the past century and a half has grown accustomed to expecting some great "Answer" to the everyday woes of life, a deliverance from the ordinary struggles of history—a "final solution," to use the odd euphemism of the Nazis concerning the so-called Jewish question. Nathaniel Hawthorne addressed the dangers inherent in this state of mind, in which human beings are tempted to surrender themselves to the vaunted claims of a heroic and "overruling purpose":

This is always true of those men who have surrendered themselves to an overruling purpose. It does not so much impel them from without, nor even operate as a motive power within, but grows incorporate with all that they think and feel, and finally converts them into little else save that one principle. . . . They have no heart, no sympathy, no reason, no conscience. They will keep no friend, unless he make himself the mirror of their purpose; they will smite and slay you, and trample your dead corpse under foot, all the more readily, if you take the first step with them, and cannot take the second, and the third, and every other step of their terribly strait path.[1]

Hawthorne, as well as others, saw in the growing spirit of revolution—a spirit that gained momentum throughout the nineteenth and into the twentieth century—enormous possibilities for idolatry, especially as the "cause" became identified with a party or a person. "They have an idol," he wrote, "to which they consecrate themselves high-priest, and deem it holy work to offer sacrifices of whatever is most precious; and never once seem to suspect—so cunning has the Devil been with them—that this false deity . . . is but the spectre of the very priest himself, projected upon the surrounding darkness."[2] Thus Hawthorne spoke of developments that would continue for most of the next century, escalating into two world wars, a forty-year cold war between international superpowers, and the period in which we now live, marked—it would seem now—by monumental struggles at many points on the globe, with no apparent dominating figure, but with fierce expectations and ruinous disappointments spiraling together into a whirlpool of political and ethnic violence.

At this moment no one dominating leader capturing international attention is likely to come to mind. There is an uncanny silence on the contemporary scene. Of course these things change quickly; tomorrow the matter may well be altogether different. But at least as I write these words, all those figures who once fit the mold of the messianic leader, who promised a new order of life for a nation or even for the world, are dead. So the contemporary world has shown a great propensity for a messiah and for messianic movements, but for now no one fills the role. Even so, it is significant that *our age shows every sign of being psychologically and socially ripe for the kinds of claims that a messiah would make.* That is because our age has not found the moral or intellectual resources that caused earlier generations to nip their

Hitlers and Stalins in the bud. We lack only the crisis and the occasion
that would make such an advent welcome to the great number who
are searching for "the Answer."

## The Gospel and the Antichrist

Our century's propensity for false messiahs doesn't mean that another
will arise, whether one like those we've already witnessed or one of
even more awesome prospect. But it may mean, especially as we seem
to be given ever more to crises on an international level, that this is
no time to ignore New Testament teachings that consistently and
strongly warn of a time of great deception calling forth a great deceiver.

In Scripture he is called antichrist when the emphasis is on his role
in opposing Christ and persecuting the faithful. The term itself is
used only in the writings of John (1 Jn 2:18, 22; 4:3; 2 Jn 7), but the
idea of the antichrist is included in Paul's teachings (2 Thess 2),
where he is called "son of perdition" and "man of lawlessness." He is
referred to as a "false messiah" or pseudo-Christ when the emphasis
is placed on the attempt to take on the role of a savior in the midst
of a crisis.

In recent years what the Gospels have to say about this matter has
been largely neglected, perhaps because Paul's comments are so extensive. At one time in the history of the church, however, these brief but
powerfully clear teachings of Jesus were extraordinarily important to
our understanding of what to anticipate and *how* the church was to
anticipate and respond to antimessianic forces. I will take note of these
teachings in a moment. First I want simply to fully impress the reader
with the great impact this whole "antichrist" prophecy has had on the
course of church history and the traditional expectation of the end
time. Later we will see why the teachings of Jesus are critical to our
understanding of the crisis to come, and to our power to discriminate
between the false and the true in the midst of crisis.

## The Personification of Evil in History

The apostle Paul's use of the term "man of lawlessness" was a way of referring to the Jewish belief that the Messiah would be opposed by a figure called Beliar. *Beliar* is rooted in a term meaning "without a yoke"—that is, without the yoke of the law.

The Jews already had in mind historical figures who fit the profile of one who would defile what is sacred, oppose what is just and seek to throw off the restraints of piety or moral duty. Antiochus IV, the Syrian-Greek ruler who desecrated the temple in Jerusalem and attempted to destroy Jewish culture in the second century B.C., would have naturally come to mind.

Early Christians identified Nero, the first Roman persecutor of the church—and in many ways the most sensationally cruel of them all—as an antichrist figure. The number 666 for the beast in Revelation is undoubtedly a cryptic way of identifying the antichrist with the dead emperor whose reputation for violence and revenge, as well as ruthless strikes against the church, were still fresh in the memories of Christians. So haunting and potent was the fear of Nero that some could not even imagine that he had actually died when he reportedly committed suicide by wounding himself in the throat. For years rumors persisted throughout the Empire that he had survived the wound and escaped across the Euphrates, or that he would return from the dead to inflict his cruelty on the people of God once again.

Nero was only the beginning. The dark dream of an antichrist so troubled the thoughts of people in both the western and eastern parts of the Empire, and in what was left of the Empire through the middle ages and on into modern times, that the label was attached to scores of others. The lands touched by Christianity, even after Islam had conquered some of these lands, never broke free of this dread vision.

Muhammad was thought by many in his time to be the antichrist. During the Reformation the papacy was often labeled antichrist—especially as it stood in contrast to the suffering humility and poverty of Christ with its Roman power, pomp and prosperity. In turn the Reformers, especially Luther, were castigated as antichrists by their most virulent opponents. Even Islamic legends took up the theme in a different form with their expectation of al-Dajjal (the deceiver), a monstrously cruel, deceitful figure who would appear shortly before the end and, many believed, would finally be slain by Jesus.

### The Vision Unsought, Unshakable

Some modern scholars would reduce this dreaded figure in prophesy to a metaphor. For instance, Bernard McGinn ended an article on the antichrist by saying that while the idea of an "individual final antichrist" continues to find expression at large, "for many Christians the antichrist has become a symbol of the evil in the human heart."[3] Modern "hermeneutics of suspicion" assumes that since there have been so many, various and disappointed efforts to identify the antichrist with a real historical figure, the whole idea must be discredited.

But why shouldn't we assume just the opposite? As dreadful as this recurring image might be, its stubborn persistence may be the way humanity has reacted to an insight that has come from extraordinarily credible sources—from the words of Jesus and from Scripture, and from the realistic assessment that evil seldom remains abstract. Who would ever have imagined the holocaust of Hitler's Nazi regime? Who can, even now, fathom the cruelty of Stalin or Mao? Even the imagination of evil in the minds of the populace at large cannot match the monstrous forms it has taken in the lives and imaginations of real individuals.

History has not taught us the impossibility of incarnate human deceit and evil; it has, especially in this last century, forced upon us its real possibility. And it has caused us to see this thing at a magnitude that we would never have otherwise believed. No century, in fact, should be more capable than this twentieth century of believing that the figure described by Jesus and the apostles could indeed arise.

Scripture allows us to think of antichrist at three levels. There is first the spirit of antichrist that is found abroad in the world. Here we have the disincarnate presence and temper of the world that opposes Christ, and that John mentions prominently. Second, we have prominent mention—in both Scripture and tradition—of the many antichrists, or false messiahs, that were present from earliest times. And then, finally, this whole prophecy of the evil opposition to the spirit of Christ comes to rest in references to one individual whose sacrilege and cruelty ultimately become the focus of these expectations. Our age can readily accept the first and perhaps the second part of these prophecies, but it finds the third more difficult. Yet Scripture cannot be fully understood without this third element: the concrete, personal and individual antichrist.

The church fathers evidently were convinced that there would be a final antichrist. All of them, with the exception sometimes of the Alexandrian fathers, expected the antichrist to be personal and individual. That did not exclude the possibility that he would be preceded by some corporate or collective manifestation of the same spirit. Nor does it deny that the spirit of antichrist might become manifest many times in many individuals. It only means that one day the choice between Christ and antichrist will be unusually clear and clearly critical. That is the day in which the world will wonder at those who choose Christ—just as the people on the streets of Nuremburg must have been appalled by those who, like Bonhoeffer, would not accept *their* savior, Adolf Hitler.

**Christ and Antichrist**
Now we turn to the teachings that have at least informed all that we know, and all we can safely speculate, about this personage from the teachings of Jesus. They are found, of course, in Mark 13 and its parallels.

Four principal points must be noted. Each helps uncover what to the early readers of the New Testament was the kernel of their end-time anticipation—the kind of anticipation that is not wasted if the end time does not arrive in one's own day. But it was the kind of anticipation, as we have seen all along, that enriches life with a vision of God's prevailing good news.

## I Am He

Jesus said to them: "Watch out that no one deceives you. Many will come in my name, claiming 'I am he,' and will deceive many." (Mk 13:5-6)

Notice that in all three Synoptic Gospels, after the disciples ask Jesus to tell them when the final events will come, his *very first words* in response are these. This tells us something quite important: Jesus himself emphasized the threat of deception by false christs.

At this point he is not yet speaking of the single figure of the end time. But he is warning of the prevalence of this tendency to imitate, and yet substitute for, the truth that he had made known in the world. And this would happen many times.

After Jesus' death and resurrection, the church did not have to wait long for a spectacular example of the very thing of which Jesus had warned. "The Fathers of the Church regarded Simon Magus as the father of all heresy," wrote Hans Jonas of an early claimant to the messianic role.[4] Magus is mentioned in Acts 8 in connection with Philip's mission in Samaria. He had already gained a following by claiming that he was the "Power of God." Accompanying him was a Phoenician woman whom he had taken from a brothel in Tyre and whom he called Helena. According to the "gospel" he preached, Helena was the "Thought of the Most High God," which had by the act of reflection become separated from the god who is the true origin of all things. Through her separation and fall, all things were created. Now he—Simon Magus, the Power of God—had come to rescue her from this low estate and thus to redeem all the earth with her. Here we see what might be considered the centerpiece of the anti-Christian substitute: the deification of humanity.

But how is this different from orthodox Christianity? you might ask. Is not the incarnation of God in Christ, this cosmic condescension of the omniscient, omnipotent and omnipresent God to the level of humanity, and the exaltation of Jesus Christ to the throne of heaven not also, in a sense, the deification and godly honoring of humankind? Was Jesus only a more convincing Simon? Both claimed identity with God. Both performed wonders and signs. Both made an enormous impact on their followers. What fair and legitimate distinction can we make?

To begin with, Jesus' exaltation was a reflection of his humiliation. Grace came through his utter subordination of his personal interest to the will of God. The cross marks the extent to which God was willing to meet humanity in redemption and the extent to which one man was willing to go in obeying God. Christianity begins with the humiliation of God, not the exaltation of humanity. It is founded on a man's hunger for godliness in obedience, not his Godlikeness in divine power.

Simon's program was not obedience to God's will but freedom from the law and power in the world. He disputed the legitimacy of moral law. According to Irenaeus, he said that

the prophets uttered their prophecies inspired by the angels that made the world [angels who were alien from the true god, and who had forgotten him—Simon being his true incarnation]; wherefore those who placed their hope in himself and Helena need no longer heed them and might freely do what they liked. For by his grace men were saved, not by righteous deeds. For works are not in their nature good [neither are they bad], but by external dispensation: the angels who made the world deeded them as such, by precepts of this kind to bring men into servitude. Wherefore he promised that the world should be dissolved and that his own should be

liberated from the dominion of those who made the world.[5]
This is good news for libertines! The emphasis on freedom from morality, the will to rise above right and wrong, stands in stark contrast
to the Christian idea of grace overcoming our separation from God
and our bondage to sin. The anti-Christian spirit means sinking deeper
into that bondage of isolation—believing that one is not really isolated
but is instead *independent* of those bothersome moral restraints. The
deceit consists in the notion that one has power, when in fact one is
only alone.

That is why Jesus first emphasizes, "Watch out that no one deceives
you."

### The Many Prophets

Many false prophets will appear and deceive many. (Mt 24:11)
False messiahs seldom appear alone. They are supported by many
highly respected voices. These are the "many prophets" who support
the general deception, making it all the more believable.

The deception brings increased isolation, enmity and hatred. The
verse announcing the false prophets is preceded by "at that time many
will turn away from the faith and will betray and hate each other" (v.
10) and is followed by "the love of most will grow cold" (v. 12). The
parallel passage in Mark includes "Brother will betray brother to
death, and a father his child. Children will rebel against their parents
and have them put to death" (Mk 13:12). Luke also speaks of the
betrayal of friends and family members.

Deception and the breakdown of society go together. Students of
history know that movements of incredibly outrageous claims and
promises broke upon the world in times of grave crisis and disorder.
In such times individuals felt the isolation of a fragmented society. Not
knowing whom to trust or what to believe, they readily fell victim to
preposterous schemes and stories that proposed to make sense of an
otherwise impossibly chaotic and senseless situation.

The mystery religions in the Roman Empire, with their weird rites of baptism in the blood of bulls and amputation of genital organs, performed in a state of wild ecstatic frenzy, seem to have caught on during the years when Rome was in imminent danger of invasion by Hannibal. The widespread genocide against Jews during the Middle Ages, excused by the preposterous story that Jews were poisoning the wells and streams of Europe, took place at the time of bubonic plagues and enormous social disorder. And as is well known, the rise of Hitler was made possible in part by the political and economic prostration of Germany. The isolation, the cultural loss of normal means of social life, the spread of violence—all of these heighten confusion and thus weaken our usual resistance to propaganda. People begin to believe things that at other times and in other places they would find utterly absurd.

Recently the Holocaust Museum was opened in Washington, D.C., amid much discussion. Some question the value of preserving such horrific memories. It is important that we do; otherwise we find the whole episode so unbelievable in our present state of mind. Such episodes of social madness do not happen frequently, and when they do happen the survivors are likely to wonder whether it was not all a bad dream. But they do happen.

So Jesus warned that a time of enormous stress, persecution and social isolation will prepare the way for a time of unprecedented deception. He returned to this warning in Matthew 24:23-24, ending with a statement that shows the magnitude of the deception. These false Christs and false prophets will "perform great signs and miracles to deceive even the elect—if that were possible."

But what makes it *not* possible for the elect? The confusion that reigns in society comes because the usual means of communicating and regulating social behavior has been disturbed. Most of us, most of the time, get our cues from society: we generally trust the messages that society gives us through its institutions, its customs, the general consensus, the media. The crisis comes when these institutions are in disarray.

But the Christian has a word uttered by Christ at the beginning of the Christian era, and it is intended to give believers a message that is reliable through every crisis, including the final one. The difference for the Christian is this: the disruption of society has not affected his or her most reliable source of truth. "See, I have told you ahead of time" (Mt 24:25). In other words, when the crisis comes it is all the more important to cling to the words of Christ himself. These words— uttered "ahead of time"—are not affected by the crisis but give stability to the Christian in the midst of utter social breakdown.

## The Abomination of Desolation

So when you see standing in the holy place "the abomination that causes desolation," spoken of through the prophet Daniel—let the reader understand—then let those who are in Judea flee to the mountains. (Mt 24:15-16)

Here Jesus' warnings come to focus on the expectations and deceptions of a single person. His words make clear reference to the prophecy in Daniel 8.

The initial object of Daniel's prophecy was Antiochus IV Epiphanes. This Syrian-Greek ruler was most remembered by Jews for having erected an altar to Zeus on the altar of the temple in Jerusalem, an object that became known as "the sacrilege that appalls," or the devastating sacrilege. There is good evidence that this altar included a statue of Zeus, whom Antiochus madly thought bore his own facial features. Thus the statue would likely have resembled Epiphanes, the "Divine Manifestation" himself. For this and other reasons his subjects often called him Epimanes, "the mad one." The attempt at self-deification would soon bring his downfall.

What must intrigue us about the reference Jesus makes to the sacrilege of Daniel's day is that the same theme was strongly played out again during Roman times. Little more than a decade after Jesus uttered these words, Caligula ordered that an image of himself as Zeus Epiphanius Neos Gaios should be fashioned and then erected at the temple in Jerusalem. The desecration was prevented, however, first because lower officials delayed placement of the statue out of fear of offending the Jews, but ultimately because of Caligula's assassination.

What sort of event stands behind, or is even prefigured, by these strange stories of rulers whose megalomania drove them to desire that their images should occupy the temple at Jerusalem? And what kind of event does Jesus' prophecy point to? We cannot be too specific here, any more than we would dare to speculate about the "day or the time" of Jesus' return. What we can see clearly is that the human desire for self-deification will come to be focused in a person of great cunning and of boundless ambition.

### The Shadow of the False Messiah
This topic presents us with a two-edged temptation. The picture we are given in the Gospels could lead us into speculation that goes far beyond the comment of Scripture. On the other hand, we can too easily dismiss the concreteness of this image and opt for a safe abstraction, reducing Jesus' clear warnings to moral advice.

I don't want to do either of these. Let me say instead that Jesus' teachings lead us to believe that he was warning of some concrete events of the end time, events that are rooted in continual human problems. We can isolate a few important points.

☐ First, the false messiah will appear at a time of great social crisis.

☐ Second, he will deceive many, even as many are willing to be deceived at a time of upheaval and uncertainty.

☐ Third, he will attempt to take the place of God, reflecting the human tendency toward self-deification.

Now, if we can safely and responsibly make any connection between these prophecies and our own time, it will be with regard to that third part of Jesus' teachings, which defines the very ground out of which the deceitfulness of the antichrist will spring. I will not say that our own time cannot be surpassed in respect to this. But I will say that no time has yet exceeded ours in preparing the minds and hearts of people for the possibility of an abomination that makes desolate: the deification of humanity.

It is the pantheism of our age—not necessarily the so-called Eastern pantheism, but the decidedly practical Western pantheism—that presents us with this new prospect of human deification. It is a short step from the opinion that my own tastes, preferences and imagination must take precedence over any outside law, tradition or authority to the conclusion that these human expressions have replaced God. And it is a shorter step still to the acceptance of the claim, in the midst of moral crisis—when people might find themselves sorely in need of a godlike authority—that an extraordinary and utterly deceitful individual can take on that role. The particular impact of pantheism on our age is a matter that I have dealt with at some length elsewhere.[6]

Let me suggest that we not engage the usual habit of following prophecy along line AB until we speculate confidently on point Z. Instead let's take time to reflect on a part of that historical line that we have all just experienced (relatively speaking) and ask what that tells us about the possibilities inherent in the modern dismantling of intellectual and affective barriers to human deification.

A book written in 1898 will help us to see how seriously one might draw the connection between pantheistic philosophies, or the deification of humanity in modern times, and the real threat of historical consequences. When Samuel J. Andrews wrote *Christianity and Anti-Christianity* in 1898, no one could have known how accurate were his misgivings about where the world was going. He wrote well before World War I, the rise of Bolshevism, Nazism, the Holocaust of World War II and the continuing trends of ideologies into our present time. By the end of the nineteenth century many had already observed a rising tide of mass movements that would earlier have been confined to fringe groups, and depended by and large on a new concept of humanity's place in the world. But only now can we see how accurately some tied the pantheistic thinking of these movements to tragic historical consequences.

Andrews traced the progress of pantheism in modern times, and he pointed to G. W. F. Hegel as the most powerful representative of that thought. Quoting John Stuart Mill, Andrews noted, "The philosophical writings of Schelling and Hegel have given pantheistic principles a complacent admission and a currency which they never before this age possessed in any part of Christendom." Already in 1857 James Buchanan had said, "The grand ultimate struggle between Christianity and atheism will resolve itself into a controversy between Christianity and pantheism." Then Andrews concluded, in his late-nineteenth-century book,

> A mighty wave of pantheism, beginning in Germany, has been sweeping over Christendom during the present century; and now finds but little to resist it. . . . It will give us a new religion based upon a new conception of God, a new Christianity based upon a new conception of Christ, a universe evolved, not created. . . . It is a religion which many will gladly welcome, for it opens a wide gate and a broad way in which all men, of whatever . . . belief, may walk without jostling one another.[7]

Where might this lead? Has history not already given us more than a primer in the kinds of desolation, and the kinds of sacrilege, that are the fruit of our present trend?

Andrews quoted Heinrich Heine (1797-1856) in a way that is startling in its prescience—and, mind you, Andrews himself could not have been aware in 1898 of the fulfillment that was to come, and that you and I know full well. Pantheistic doctrines, Heine wrote, "have developed revolutionary forces which only await the day to break forth and fill the world with terror, and with punishment." He continued with special emphasis on Germany:

> Should that subduing talisman, the Cross, break, then will come crashing and roaring forth the world-madness of the old champions, the insane Berserker rage. . . . That talisman is brittle, and the day will come when it will pitifully break[!] . . . Thought goes before the deed, and lightning precedes thunder. German thunder will come, and ye will hear it crash as naught ever crashed before in the whole history of the world. . . . Then will be played in Germany a drama, compared to which the French Revolution will be only an innocent idyll. Just now all is tolerably quiet. The great actors have not yet appeared upon the stage, the great army of gladiators. The hour will come.[8]

Now that the hour has come—and gone, will we witness a drama on the world scene of even greater calamity and consequence? Will the scale of suffering exceed Hitler's Holocaust and Stalin's murders, even as these eclipsed the French Revolution?

If so, how shall we endure? Jesus did not leave that question unanswered.

# 7

# The Holy Spirit
# & the Last Days

*Whenever you are arrested and brought
to trial, do not worry beforehand
about what to say. Just say whatever
is given you at the time,
for it is not you speaking,
but the Holy Spirit.*

*(MARK 13:11)*

W HEN I KNEW DAVID LI, HE WAS A BAPTIST SEMINARY
student in Taipei, Taiwan. He had grown up in a family with animistic
beliefs. Spirits and ghosts inhabited the nooks and crannies of their
world and watched somehow from the realm of the dead. When his
father died, a reign of terror seized the household. In death, the father
was no cherished memory but a threatening and violent presence. The
mother's fears of ruin and starvation added to the family's general
state of anxiety. "We are all going to die!" she kept telling her five
small children.

One day, David Li's mother took up a Chinese-language New Testament that a missionary had given her. As she turned to the Gospel
of John, her eyes fell upon Jesus' promise to send "another Comfort-
er." The passage included words translated literally in Chinese, even
though most English versions at the time were not literal. It said, "I
will not leave you as orphans" (Jn 14:18).

She read on, wanting to know more about this Savior who would
not leave his disciples "orphans" and this God who provided for the
orphans of the world. "When my mother believed in Jesus," David

said later, "a peace we had never known came to my family."

The passage that spoke so strongly to the heart of this desperate mother is thought by some students of the New Testament to represent a later "reinterpretation" of the Christian hope. The argument runs like this: Since the parousia had not occurred and it was now a long time that Christians had expected it, they eventually took the Second Coming to mean life in the Spirit. So the church turned from its early intense expectation to an adaptability and almost a contentment with this status quo.

But nothing could be further from the flavor of these teachings on the Holy Spirit in the Gospels. In the Synoptic Gospels and John, nearly every mention of the coming and abiding Spirit is made in connection with conflict, tension and persecution. This connection is highly significant. It shows how inseparable is the idea of the Holy Spirit from the expectation of an inescapable conflict. Yet fundamentally Jesus' saying is rooted in the fact that the Holy Spirit addresses the crisis with a hope that transcends both the conflict and *the methods of conflict.*

### The Conflict and the Witness of the Spirit

The peace that the Holy Spirit gives involves both the believer and the world in a huge paradox.

In all three of the Synoptic Gospels we read Jesus' warnings that his followers will be delivered to courts, flogged in the synagogues, dragged before governors and kings, and put in prison. All races of people will put them to death. The pressure against Christians will be so great that many will deny their faith, betray others and hate others—even those within their own families (Mt 24:9-11; Mk 13:9-13; Lk 21:12-17).

At the same time the persecutors of these Christians will believe themselves to be "offering a service to God" (Jn 16:2). The gospel antagonizes. It appears to be not a message of peace but the very cause of conflict. No doubt the lives of late-first-century Asian Christians, suffering the flame of Roman persecution, would have been decidedly more peaceful in one sense if they had never heard the gospel. And no doubt late-twentieth-century Christians will drift more peacefully into a neopagan night if they never take the gospel seriously. To the world at large, the peace that the Christian speaks of can look like conflict, resistance and war.

### The Secular Peace Agenda

We can best understand the world's view of this if we consider how the world usually pursues peace. Just as "nature abhors a vacuum," societies seem to abhor chaos and disorder. If they cannot have harmony, they'll settle for conflict—a conflict in which the enemy is written out of the human race and allies are closer than brothers. Conflict, in fact, is often preferred to peace. It clarifies things. Friend and foe are never more sharply defined. Comrades in a great struggle are often more cherished than are mere neighbors in peacetime.

When is this kind of clarity and camaraderie most needed?

Notice that the prophecies of Jesus speak not only of persecution but also of a variety of natural and social calamities. Luke writes of the increasing tensions of society breaking out in warfare, *along with* natural disasters, famines and plagues (21:9-11). These natural calamities increase the centrifugal forces that pull society apart, increasing suspicion, isolation, uncertainty and discouragement.

René Girard, the Stanford literary critic and philosopher, has shown how persecution arises out of the uncertainty of social chaos. Societies in danger resort to what he calls the "scapegoat mechanism."[1] Under pressure of natural disasters, disease or economic collapse, individuals become isolated and feel themselves victims of inexplicable misfortune; their former habits of civility and mutual trust dwindle and sometimes disappear. In such circumstances there is a strong temptation to single out a scapegoat. The scapegoat is a person or group who is seen as distinct in some way from the larger community. Scapegoats are outsiders. Once the scapegoat is identified, the community begins to reconstitute itself around the cause of *persecuting the scapegoat*. Thus, as Girard explains, the rising incidence of mutual violence and the loss of community are overcome by the identification and persecution of a common enemy. Further, since the scapegoat is always an individual or a minority group, it cannot strike back. In one stroke, society has restored its own harmony without facing the perils of warfare.

Usually the idea that the scapegoat might be responsible for all of a society's problems is preposterous. Medieval Jews in Europe, for instance, were not responsible for the bubonic plague. Yet often they were killed by the hundreds even before the plague reached a city. The idea of the scapegoat is first of all a lie. But people will cooperate in lies for the sake of strengthening community. When calamity threatens, the thought of isolation and chaos is more unendurable than even the original threat. Individuals sense the need for a society marked by cooperation and solidarity. This is most important at a time of crisis. A bit of self-deception may seem a small price to pay, even when it draws the community into collective murder.

The scapegoat response also tells us another thing. When given a choice, people prefer to overwhelm their problems, to exercise power or control over them, to locate the source of the problem and root it out. That, of course, is not surprising. But when the problem is greater than anyone can control, such as a plague or natural disaster, we still prefer to believe that the solution is within our grasp. Out of fright, we will not permit ourselves to believe that we have no power over this matter; instead we convince ourselves that someone is at fault, and thus the solution to the problem is at hand.

Medieval Europeans could not stop the plague, but they could murder Jews. And if everyone was saying that this desperate slaughter of innocents was striking at the root of the problem, an individual might well quiet his disturbing suspicions that the whole business was absurd. In such a situation mob mentality takes over, and collective murder temporarily calms the troubled waters.

Could Christians come to be on the receiving end of this scapegoating? It's well to remember that we have a classic example in Nero's persecution of Christians in the first century. The calamity that threatened Roman society was a huge fire that destroyed much of the city. As the Roman historian Tacitus explained, Nero was desperate to calm the anger and turmoil of the citizenry. Christians became the scapegoats. And though Nero's inventive cruelty later generated some popular sympathy for the courageous Christians, at first he accomplished his purpose. The troubles of a city in crisis found their target, and peace was restored.

Since the third century, Christians have frequently been in the majority, especially in the West. And, to their shame, they were on many occasions the persecutors, denying their own first principles. Now, in what is often called a post-Christian world, we have come full circle. Christians are increasingly isolated. As James Dobson pointed out on his radio broadcast, "Christians are the only group that [is] unfashionably in the minority" (*Focus on the Family,* February 4, 1994).

It is coincidentally interesting that in the United States, the country with the largest Christian population, the most decidedly Christian group is African-American. Thus post-Christian America includes a group of people who constitute a conspicuous minority on two counts! How significant this is we cannot yet know. We have not recently witnessed the kind of social catastrophe that generally propels communities into a state of mob psychosis. But it is almost too much to hope that it will never come. It is intriguing to contemplate the possibility that the church of the end time might discover that the success of its witness to Christ depends strongly on its solidarity with brothers and sisters who are of a minority race in many post-Christian nations.

When persecution does come (Jesus' words do not permit an *if*), we cannot forget that this is always the world's route to "peace." As "peace," it is also the logical extension of condemnation and persecution. Every despot intuitively knows the trick. It is a kind of peace that summons the demons of violence to its aid.

## Peace as Promise of the Spirit

What is the Christian alternative to "peace through persecution"? The world resorts to lies, accusation, coercion, violence and collective murder. But what else is left when the world itself seems ready to fly apart? This is the direct question to which Jesus' teachings respond.

What is left, indeed, is the truth! Perhaps we should try that for a change, since we've tried everything else. This is where Jesus' saying on the Spirit leads us.

Mark's words take us from the witness of the Spirit to the witness of truth-telling believers: "Whenever you are arrested and brought to trial, do not worry beforehand what to say. Just say whatever is given you at the time, for it is not you speaking, but the Holy Spirit" (Mk 13:11).

Look carefully. Does this mean that disciples will overwhelm their persecutors with arguments that come from God? Not exactly. As we know, in times of persecution Christians have not experienced victory in the ordinary sense at all. They have become martyrs, which is to say they were killed. They suffered for Christ by the hundreds. The word *martyr* is Greek for "witness." Early Christians were using a wonderful euphemism here: to be killed for Christ is to bear testimony for him. As Luke records it, Jesus said, "They will lay hands on you and persecute you. . . . This will result in your being witnesses [martyrs] to them" (21:12-13). They stood over against the *appearance* of the present and gave witness to the truth of God's future.

In his three-volume *The Gulag Archipelago* Aleksandr Solzhenitsyn chronicled the horrors of the Soviet regime from Lenin and Stalin on up to the 1970s. The question: How might people loosen the grip of a system so iron-strong and so lacking in human sympathies? His answer was unvarying: Stop cooperating in, and believing, the lie. One day, as we know, that happened. The lie could no longer be believed, and the system collapsed like a house of cards. Suddenly what had seemed a great immovable power in the midst of the earth vanished, leaving (as it seemed from this distance) little eddies of chaos and uncertainty where once had stood the regime that for most of a century convinced many people that it held "the future."

This ultimate failure of evil, in spite of its apparent success, is the truth that the world itself cannot tell us. The Holy Spirit bears witness, bringing us assurance of things to come—that the truth of God is the ultimate triumph of good. "And we know that in all things God works for the good of those who love him, who have been called according to his purpose," wrote the apostle Paul (Rom 8:28). That is not a fact that one gains from experience in the world, but a truth that declares knowledge of the end of all things in God.

### The Gospels and the Spirit's Promise

Let's see how this principle of peace, that we have already seen in its remarkable contrast to the world's normal method of restoring order, is impressed upon us by the Gospels—first the Synoptics and then John.

In the Synoptics we find that (1) the Holy Spirit is always mentioned in association with the tendency to encounter condemnation and (2) the nature of the Spirit of God is to answer evil with good. In every crisis and every conflict, it is the Spirit who answers with blessing, while the bent of evil, or the Evil One, is to curse.

The first reference to the Spirit comes in the account of the birth of John, whom the angel announces will be "filled with the Holy Spirit even from birth" (Lk 1:15). Where there is conflict and alienation he will bring reconciliation, turning the people back to their God, parents back to their children, and the disobedient back to their right mind (vv. 16-17).

The other early references have to do with the pregnancy of Mary, who is in a situation normally condemned by the community and who might expect condemnation by her espoused husband. Instead, since it is by the Holy Spirit that she has conceived (Mt 1:20; Lk 2:35), she is blessed by Elizabeth, who is "filled with the Holy Spirit," and by Simeon, who after the birth is moved by the Spirit to prophecy about the conflict in which Mary has, by virtue of her election by the Spirit, become a part. "This child is destined to cause the falling and rising of many in Israel, and to be a sign that will be spoken against, so that the thoughts of many hearts will be revealed. And a sword will pierce your own soul too" (Lk 2:34-35).

The pattern of conflict with evil and the Spirit's consistent blessing in that conflict is seen next in the account of Jesus' baptism and the temptation that follows. John's announcement of Jesus predicts that one will appear who will baptize not with water (the baptism of repentance and personal death) but with the Holy Spirit—that is, with life. The baptism itself is a sign of Jesus' willing death and his resurrected life. It is a sign, that is, of the conflict that will be the focus and result of his life. As the Holy Spirit descends visibly in the form of a dove—which recalls the dove of a renewed world peace after Noah's flood—we read the Father's blessing: "You are my Son, whom I love; with you I am well pleased" (Mk 1:11; Lk 3:22; compare Mt 3:17).

Immediately, however, we find the Spirit of God does not augur peace *without* conflict, but that he promises precisely a peace that overcomes conflict. So it is the Spirit who at once "sent [Jesus] out into the desert," where his contest with Satan took place. This association of Spirit with temptation or "test" should remind us instantly of Matthew's text that warns, "Do not suppose that I have come to bring peace to the earth. I did not come to bring peace, but a sword" (Mt 10:34). This association is all the more remarkable when we realize that it occurs within the context of a series of teachings that includes the saying that disciples should not "worry about what to say or how to say it, . . . for it will not be you speaking, but the Spirit of your Father speaking through you" (Mt 10:19-20).

Jesus' appearance in Nazareth, recorded in Luke, is especially instructive when we view the text carefully. He returns to Galilee ("in the power of the Spirit"—Lk 4:14) and reads to the synagogue in Nazareth from the Isaiah prophecy. It is the prophecy that begins:

The Spirit of the Lord is on me,
  because he has anointed me
  to preach good news to the poor.
He has sent me to proclaim freedom for the prisoners
  and recovery of sight for the blind,
  to release the oppressed,
  to proclaim the year of the Lord's favor. (Lk 4:18-19)

Here Jesus ends the reading, saying, "Today this Scripture is fulfilled in your hearing" (v. 21). However, a glance at Isaiah 61:1-2 will show us that he stopped, significantly, midphrase! The next words—the words that most certainly were left out by design—were "and the day of vengeance of our God."

Thus the text from Isaiah speaks of the great blessing of the people of God and at the same time tells of the judgment of God's enemies. Yet Jesus' role is not judgment here, but blessing and life for those who are oppressed and afflicted. His role is always good news and not condemnation and revenge. John's Gospel, as usual, expresses this concept directly and explicitly: "For God did not send his Son into the world to condemn the world, but to save the world through him" (Jn 3:17). The vengeance and condemnation do come—but they come not as a result of the Spirit's work, which is always a work of love, but because of human refusal of that love. "Light has come into the world, but men loved darkness instead of light because their deeds were evil" (Jn 3:19)—this is the condemnation. The "vengeance of God" is that God will not force men and women to accept his love;

but the conflict between God and humanity arises from the fact that God has offered it.

## Judgment Is Salvation Refused

One afternoon recently a group of students tried desperately to save a small duckling that had fallen into a drainpipe at the edge of a campus pond. Each time they tried to retrieve the duck, it would swim away out of fear of its would-be rescuers. There were enormous efforts to save the duckling, a great elaborate scheme of the sort that only college students are likely to devise; there was ingenuity enough to qualify for a credit-hour in physics; and at last there was a great hue and cry over the duck's predicament. All to no avail. The duck would not be saved.

God has offered life and blessing. Now we must choose. That is the crisis that Jesus sent forth in the world. It is always, ultimately, a crisis of the end time, an eschatological crisis, because the day will come when the choice has been made. Already. It will be the day of consequences—the day of "the vengeance of our God."

The victory of Jesus is expressed as a victory over Satan. When Jesus sends out the seventy-two disciples, and they return having taken out the message of the kingdom of God, he exults, "I saw Satan fall like lightning from heaven" (Lk 10:18). Luke is careful to say that Jesus is, at the time, "full of the Holy Spirit" (v. 21), thus emphasizing that the blessing of the Spirit prevails in the midst of the conflict. The mention of Satan here is especially significant when we realize that the meaning of *Satan* in the language of Jesus is "the accuser." This role of Satan as the one who accuses and condemns, the one who gives full expression to worldly rebellion against God, the refusal of his gift of love, throws into relief what we have consistently seen about the role of the Holy Spirit in the eschatological conflict.

In our courts—a system inherited from the Romans—a counselor for the defense makes the best case possible for the one who is being accused of wrongdoing. The defense lawyer's words are calculated to emphasize the virtue and innocence of the accused. Over against the defender is the prosecutor—the accuser—who tries to expose the defendant's guilt and prove the accused's wanton tendency toward evil. What we have seen in the Gospels, so far, is that the role of the Holy Spirit corresponds to that of an attorney for the defense. Only he argues for the *ultimate* and eschatological guiltlessness of the human being. He sees the loved one not simply as is—unfinished and incomplete, still burdened by the bondage of sin—but as the person will be when God has finally had his way. And his argument is that *God will have his way.*

On the other side is the accuser. The reality of Satan is always evident in the individual or society living in contradiction to itself—turned against itself. The accuser argues for condemnation. He is aided by the reality of sin—a condition he argues is unavoidable, natural and thus the ultimate and final word about the accused. He defends sin as inevitable and views the sinner as inevitably fated to sin. That the sin isolates the sinner, holds the sinner in bondage and ultimately causes the death of the sinner is no cause for concern. For the accuser's interest is condemnation. His goal is death.

It seems that thinking about the Spirit in relation to the end forces us to a profound simplicity. In the end we have chosen life or death. It is God who contends for our life; sin and Satan contend for our death.

### The Paraclete and the End Time
If this "simplified" reading of the Gospels has any integrity, however, we should be able to discover somewhere that the point is made expressly. As a matter of fact we are able to do so. We find the point in the writings of John, the most theologically reflective of the Evangelists.

First, we find that the Holy Spirit is referred to in John's Gospel as the Paraclete, sometimes translated "counselor." *Paraclete* is a transliterated rendering of the Greek *paraklētos,* which has precisely the same meaning as the Latin *advocatus,* "advocate." While Jesus came into the world, John said, not "to condemn the world, but to save the world" (Jn 3:17), he also pledged to send another Paraclete *(allon paraklēton)* like him, who would "be with you forever" (Jn 14:16). Thus the gift of God is to be an everlasting advocate for each of us.

This power and intention of God to speak and act for us differs radically from the ways of the world. God has ultimately settled the case in our favor. The world still attempts to settle matters in a spirit of conflict and conquest, using power and prestige to overwhelm enemies, and even friends and family members who have inadvertently become competitors. With the sending of the Paraclete, Jesus pronounces peace, but not the peace that the world gives (Jn 14:27). For the peace that the world gives means being temporarily on the winning side. The world is full of struggles, violence and revenge on different levels; its system is made up of a certain balance—always and only for the moment—in the contest to survive. The best the world can offer is that we may prevail for the moment.

The world's peace is that of the young athlete who has not yet lost his youth, the aged financier who has not yet lost his health, the corporate executive whose position and prestige are eyed hungrily by those in the junior ranks. It is the peace of the "better" side of town, unaware of the rising tide of violence among those a few blocks away who are kept quiet by public programs and hopelessness. It is the expectant quiet of a lit fuse.

The peace of the world is always fragile, always under threat, always being lost and never gained in any ultimate sense. For it is always gained at the expense of someone else; it is the fruit of envy and ambition as well as resignation and despair. It is the peace that exists between the victorious and the vanquished, the winners and the losers, the haves and the have-nots, the powerful and the powerless—a peace always bearing the seeds of envy and revenge, along with the promise of future struggles and a new and different, but still fragile, peace.

A peace "not as the world gives" means justification offered to all, out of reach of none. It means a hope for things eternal in preference to things temporal. It means competing only in the sense of trying to "outdo one another in good works." A peace "not as the world gives" means building a community on the basis of mutual forgiveness, rather than a fragile alliance based on common enemies or a common threat. It is a peace based on mercy rather than judgment.

This other idea of peace sounds commonplace. It *is* commonplace as an idea. The gospel has made it commonplace. But as a reality, it remains a mystery of which we have only occasional glimpses.

The apocalyptic doctrine of the Holy Spirit begins with the prophecy that one day the veil will be torn from top to bottom. The deception of the former "worldly" peace will be revealed. And all will see that the true peace of God, the peace that from the foundation of the world lay hidden, was disclosed only in the crucified Christ—the God of self-giving love. But glimpses of this greater reality have been seen all along since that time, and this has been the work of the Holy Spirit. It is he who cares for orphans, reminding them that they do, after all, have a Father.

# 8

# Remembrance
# of Things to Come

*But in those days, following that distress,*
*"the sun will be darkened,*
*and the moon will not give its light;*
*the stars will fall from the sky,*
*and the heavenly bodies will be shaken."*

*At that time men will see the Son of Man*
*coming in clouds with great power and glory.*
*And he will send his angels and gather*
*his elect from the four winds, from the ends*
*of the earth to the ends of the heavens.*

*Now learn this lesson from the fig tree:*
*As soon as its twigs get tender*
*and its leaves come out, you know*
*that summer is near. Even so, when you see*
*these things happening, you know that it is near,*
*right at the door. I tell you the truth,*
*this generation will certainly not pass away*
*until all these things have happened.*
*Heaven and earth will pass away,*
*but my words will never pass away.*

*(MARK 13:24-31)*

*I*N ICELAND LAST SPRING, FIGURLAUG INGVARSDOTTIR SPOTTED an object tossing in the surf near her home at the mouth of the Vididals River. She retrieved a dark bottle, perfectly sealed with wax, and drew from it a note, written apparently by an English-speaking child named Stewart. She took the note to a friend, a radio announcer, who could read English. Her friend, in turn, contacted others in the media and began the search for Stewart.

Such things do happen occasionally. From ancient times young scribblers at the beach for a holiday have dropped a note into a bottle, sealed it up and tossed the capsule end over end, in a great arc, into the ocean surf. Perhaps one day, each imagined, some beachcomber in a faraway place and time would find the bottle and read those very words. Not often, but frequently enough to make it plausible, someone like this Icelandic shepherd's wife finds the bottle. When it's found it's a bit like a miracle.

The note from Stewart was sent from Charleston, South Carolina. "I hope," he wrote, "someone will get this letter in a faraway land like France or Denmark." In spite of the publicity in South Carolina and Iceland, the writer was never found. That's not surprising, for the note was dated "9 October 1982"—eleven years earlier. Marine scientists speculated that the bottle was caught up into the strong currents of the Gulf Stream and that it circulated tens of thousands of miles through the Atlantic before coming to rest more than a decade after it was launched.

People are naturally awestruck by such discoveries. What perils the bottle must have passed through! What distances it traveled! What a slim chance that it would fall into the hands of this young woman on this particular day, so far from the warm Carolina coast, or that the world would ever hear of it!

Yet the words printed at the head of this chapter have come through greater perils, traveled amazing distances and washed up on the shores of every land. And, further, there is a self-consciousness about this destiny embedded in the words themselves: "Heaven and earth will pass away, but my words will never pass away" (v. 31). The words are tossed out in this remote corner of the world, but in due time—at the right time—they will come to you.

For these are words about the end of time, and they are therefore words about the *meaning* of time. The real purpose of anything cannot be truly and completely known until the end of everything. Everything finds its value in its end; its true purpose is revealed in its conclusion.

### The Power of the Future over the Present

In a couple of weeks I expect to attend a meeting near Baltimore. Meanwhile I will be following a schedule of events that will probably make no sense to anyone not knowing my purpose. I must make certain adjustments in my schedule of classes, grade papers at a faster-than-ordinary clip, skip a few of the faculty coffee klatches and change some appointments. None of these things will get me any closer to Baltimore, and they make sense only insofar as the end result is a trip to this meeting. In fact, as I get closer to the time of the meeting, more and more of my activity will be determined or "ruled" by those plans in my immediate future. How many times do our present actions make sense only after we know their purpose, their goal, their *telos?*

The Bible, as many have noticed, is extraordinarily interested in the end of things. You might just as well say it is engaged with the *meaning* of things, or the *purpose* of things. The end of life, and the end of the world itself, will disclose something—either the utter futility of existence or some sort of purposefulness.

In the Bible, the end or purpose of things is often related to the idea that God's presence will finally be evident in all things. That sense is carried in the word *glory—kāḇôḏ* in the Old Testament, *doxa* in the New Testament. The gospel is gospel—that is, good news—because it tells us that all this common life is touched by a glory, a destiny with God.

### Remembering the Certainty of the End

Jesus lived, as we do, in a world largely unaware of its end or its destination. Jerusalem was unwilling to be warned or comforted because it could not see the desolation it soon faced (Mt 23:37). The teachings of Jesus could be seen as remarkable in one sense because they raised people's minds to a level of intense consciousness concerning the end time of world history—not the *time* of the end, but the *fact* of the end time.

It shouldn't surprise us that wherever early Christian believers were found there were also real and imminent end-time expectations. The reason that it shouldn't surprise us is not, however, that Jesus and the apostles predicted any immediate end; there is every evidence that they warned against predictions of that sort. The Gospels, Acts and the letters of Paul are consistent on this question: "No one knows about that day or hour, not even the angels in heaven, nor the Son, but only the Father" (Mt 24:36).

The reason this intense and even imminent expectation shouldn't surprise us is that the force and absolute focus on the end time in the teachings of both Jesus and the apostles had a very strong effect on their followers' experience of time. That is, time and the temporal world were seen all the more as having a very fragile hold upon reality. The glory of God in his ultimate disclosure at the end time shone so intensely on the things of this world that they became transparent to that glory. Whether brief or not, the mere duration of the world's existence seemed to matter less when the temporal nature of all things was so powerfully apparent.

I will always remember a conversation I had with Warren Batts, a deacon in my church who had been converted at age fifty. Recalling the early days of his Christian life, he said he was expecting Christ to "come out of the skies at any moment." "Every day I thought it might happen," he said. Now, Warren Batts was a serious student of the Bible. He knew intellectually that "no one knows about that day or hour." But the point was nonetheless clear to him: all things fade in their partial and transitory nature before the blazing reality of the perfect, ultimate, end-time return of Christ.

It is not, of course, that our time—that is, our present experience— is made empty and meaningless by this expectation of an overpowering apocalyptic future, like the experience of a boy who suddenly loses interest in his balloon when he sees a blimp. Instead, present time is given a new perspective, its true perspective, and therefore the present is made relevant to the end. The Roman Empire was transformed by Christianity precisely because Christians saw Rome no longer as "Eternal Rome" but as a city that would one day come to an end. As Tertullian said to the third-century despisers of Christianity, Christians behaved like others in civic, social and commercial life, "abjuring neither forum, nor shambles, nor bath, nor booth, nor workshop, nor inn, nor weekly market. ... We sail with you, and fight with you, and till the ground with you." The difference consisted in this: this is your home, but we are on a "sojourn with you in the world."[1]

Peter recognized the danger of Christians' losing this sense of the ultimate when they are caught up in the continuing, day-by-day course of the world in time. He wrote, "But do not forget this one thing, dear friends: With the Lord a day is like a thousand years, and a thousand years are like a day" (2 Pet 3:8). The more one is impressed with the reality of eternity and the certainty of the end, the more one becomes indifferent to the length of time that the world can claim for itself. That does not make one indifferent to the world; it only makes one aware of the world as it really is, bounded by time and certain to end.

Along with the hope of eternity, this thought rang like a firebell through the dark night of Rome's collapse. Only the gospel made it possible for some in that Empire to experience this fact as hope rather than as despair.

### Remembering the Hope of the End

If there is hope in Jesus' teachings, however, we must find it in the midst of some terrifying predictions. Jesus had given notice to his disciples that they would face deception (Mk 13:5-6 and parallels), alarming international conflict and natural disasters (vv. 7-8), persecution (vv. 9-11), betrayal (vv. 12-13), blasphemy and idolatry (v. 14). The turning point in Mark's account comes at verse 24: "But in those days, following that distress, . . . men will see the Son of Man coming in clouds with great power and glory" (vv. 24-26). What follows is Christ's promise that the distress will end and the Son of Man will triumph over the days of evil.

These prophecies have a strange quality about them that is often overlooked. There is a sense of immediacy about them—not an immediacy that could be taken as urgency, the way Albert Schweitzer tended to read the Gospels, but a directness. They embody a call to discipline, with a strong *second-person* pattern of speech. Jesus is not speaking as if these are distant, speculative matters that he and the apostles discuss in an hour of leisure. His manner of speech is I-Thou:

I call *you*.

I charge *you*.

I warn *you*.

I am making *you* responsible.

Jesus speaks directly, not indirectly; in the second person, not the third person. "When will these things take place?" the disciples ask. He answers, "Watch out that no one deceives you" (Mk 13:5). "Do not [you] follow them . . . do not be frightened" (Lk 21:8-9). "You must be on your guard. You will be handed over to the local councils . . . you will stand before governors and kings. . . . Whenever you are arrested . . . just say whatever is given you. . . . Men will hate you. . . . I have told you everything" (Mk 13:9, 11, 13, 23).

We have a clear sense that events are about to overtake these very disciples who are with Jesus. In fact, Jesus himself will be the first to travel the path. Yet he is also speaking about events whose timetable he claims not to know. The events that are about to overtake those standing on the Mount of Olives will one day overtake the world. Like King Lear, these disciples are about to "enter into the mystery of things."

Now, if what I have just said properly describes the tenor of Jesus' words—a sense of immediacy coupled with an indefiniteness about the fulfillment of these things—that gives us a clue as to how we might read them.

## Memory and Anticipation

Very soon—in a matter of days, in fact—Jesus' words would not only be predictions of the end of history; they would become for the apostles also a memory—a memory not only of his teachings but also of the immediate crisis that faced Jesus in those days. And as a memory of very definite historical events, foreshadowing the great end of all history, the words became a guide for the call to discipleship. To recapture this sense of the passage, we must read these words on three levels.

First, the prophecies clearly suggest what the disciples were about to see for themselves: the persecution, the signs within nature, the deception, the betrayal, the death-dealing of Christ's enemies and finally the ultimate triumph of Christ. All of these things happened and were fulfilled in the passion and the resurrection of Jesus. In a way, Jesus' earliest disciples were to see the whole career of a world caught between its own rebellion and God's redemption—a career that was foreordained, as well as foreshadowed, in the cross and resurrection of Christ.

Notice particularly these words appearing in all the Synoptics: "I tell you the truth, this generation will not pass away until all these things have happened" (Mk 13:30; Mt 24:34; Lk 21:32). If this saying is only about the end of history, then it becomes most difficult to understand—unless we simply think that Jesus was mistaken and that the early church, even while preserving the record of these words, chose to ignore that fact. Understanding them as referring to the passion and resurrection of Jesus, however, is strongly related to the way the church initially responded to the gospel. That is, the events in the life of Jesus—especially in his death and resurrection—are fulfillments of these end-time expectations.

In short, the death and resurrection of Jesus, accompanied as they were with cosmic and historic signs, brought the reality of the ultimate future into the midst of history. The judgment of humanity, the resurrection of the dead and the new creation are embodied in the events of Jesus' own suffering and glory. Thus for the early Christians the ultimate destiny of the world had already been staked out. They knew where the world was going because they remembered it; they had already seen it. The fact that God would prevail, and that the best efforts of evil to overcome would fail, was no longer in question. They had witnessed the final crisis, and they knew its outcome.

They had good news for the world, because they would remember the future.

On the second level, we are correct in taking these words to refer to the "end of the age" or the "end of the world." The full and final triumph of God over sin and evil will occur then.

On yet a third level, these words refer to every occasion of distress, persecution, betrayal and temptation to be faced by those who belong to Christ. The words powerfully evoke this conviction: "Remember, *these* things come to an end. The evil and pain you face seem the greatest reality as long as they last, but when the end of the struggle comes, you will see that it did not overcome you; and when these things end you will find that the Son of Man, to whom you cling, is still there. His appearance was near, you see, for it took only the end of the struggle for his presence to be made evident." He was there all along. "Even so, when you see these things happening, you know that it is near, right at the door." *What* was near? The triumph of God, the end of evil, the coming kingdom.

So the words always point to the end (the second meaning), and their truth is fully manifested in God's vindication of Jesus over the cross and the grave (the first meaning). In these two, the point is made that evil will ultimately fail and that God's mercy and goodness will prevail. But the application of this teaching is found in the third meaning. It is the struggle against evil as a daily experience—with more infrequent times of great testing—that brings these teachings to life. It is the desire to live by faith, made possible because the Christian

trusts in the faithfulness of God. That is what these words signify—
the full reliability of God, proved in the resurrection and promised in
the return of Christ. The New Testament witnesses to the fact that
God's promise of the ultimate and end-time triumph of good over evil
is no longer an abstraction hidden in heaven or removed to the remote
future, but it has been accomplished concretely in history. It is therefore a certainty, made certain in the life, death and resurrection of
Christ.

Now there is nothing to fear, because we have already seen the
outcome. Our actions, if based on faith, can conform to the truth that
has already been demonstrated, the truth that evil will ultimately fail
and good will ultimately endure.

In the midst of a pitched battle, the outcome often seems uncertain.
From moment to moment, depending on circumstances, hearts rise to
the occasion or courage utterly fails. Despair and hope change places
with every turn in the tide of battle. But if one has already seen the
end, and if the outcome is certain because the future has invaded
history in the form of Jesus' resurrection, then for those who believe,
the battle is already theirs even while they struggle.

This powerfully significant disclosure changed the world. It also
bore the power to continue working a change on the world. In a world
ruled by habit and tradition, Jesus turned the perspective around.
From this point on, tradition, laws and customs, as well as philosophies and social manners, would begin to be anchored in the future.
But they were anchored not in plans or wishes for the future; they were
anchored instead in the remembrance of a future that had already been
revealed by God.

### The Dialectic of Past and Future
Here in Charleston, South Carolina, old houses and memories of old
events are sometimes cherished and sometimes considered a hindrance
to progress. Every community, not just this one, relates in some way

to its past. So do individuals and groups. Some view the past as a refuge from a bewildering and threatening future. Others attempt to escape responsibility for the past by fleeing to a rootless and forgetful future. Either way can be destructive. The Christian gospel neither hopes without remembering nor remembers without hoping. Rather, it draws on the past in order to anticipate the future. Instituting the Lord's Supper, Jesus said, "Do this in remembrance of me" (Lk 22:19). But the memory anticipated a further fellowship: "I will not eat it again until it finds fulfillment in the kingdom of God" (v. 16). The possibility of remembering God's future prompted Peter to increase the hope of the persecuted church by giving believers "reminders to stimulate you to wholesome thinking," over against those who are scoffers, following their contemporary and narrow appetites and saying, "Where is this 'coming' he promised?" (2 Pet 3:1, 3). Those who followed Jesus, however, brought into the world a new kind of memory, a new relationship of past and future. No longer was the future ruled by the past. Now it was the other way around. For these people had witnessed the resurrection of the dead. Now the glory of God's future ruled the present and even stirred the ashes of the dead past. For now it was understood that all things that had ever happened were taken up into the ultimate triumph of God. The judgment of the world had taken place and would take place. The triumph of Christ had taken place and would yet take place.

**False and True Choices About the Future**
There is a dreary kind of fatalism that comes to rest in a world that thinks (as the pagan world must) that it has no appeal from the past. The past, in this way of thinking, has an absolute grip on the future. Robert Frost's "The Road Not Taken" speaks of this anxiety over a fundamental and irrevocable life choice. Two roads lie before us at once:

And both that morning equally lay

In leaves no step had trodden black.
Oh, I kept the first for another day!
Yet knowing how way leads to way,
I doubted if I should ever come back.[2]

Christians are often troubled by whether they might have irrevocably made the wrong choice. I might reason predictably from a Christian perspective that not only is my own judgment compromised by sin, but the limits of creatureliness keep me from knowing what I need to know in order to make the right decision. Painfully, I might come to realize that I could one day (with Frost) be "telling this with a sigh"—that I chose one way rather than the other.

A friend in Missouri, whom I know to be a genuine Christian witness with an influence on young people beyond anything he probably even realizes, told me of his anguish over having chosen a career in college sports rather than in pastoral ministry. He sent me a copy of a poem he had once written in the throes of loss and regret—a poem entitled "What Might Have Been."

Coming upon this poem again recently, I realized how very courageous it was for him to wrestle so forthrightly with these feelings and deeply painful doubts. And I realized what pain and what deep psychological anguish this dread of having taken the wrong path must cause many people—especially, perhaps, Christians who have a strong sense of duty before God.

Sometimes the pain has less to do with a vocational choice than with the commission of a sin, which is then seen as an irrevocable denial of a place in God's plan for each of our lives.

The gospel bears upon this dilemma, and this very human anxiety, in an important way. Rightly understood, it inexorably pulls Christian sentiment away from the pagan notion of the tyranny of the past. Because now, as we see in light of the resurrection, the past does not altogether determine the future, but it is the other way around. The future colors and shapes the present and even invades the past. David's adultery with Bathsheba and his murderous plot against her husband—condemned by God, and judged through endless strife in David's family—was nevertheless forgiven. David and Bathsheba's subsequent marriage, it is important to see, was not annulled but was even honored. This same marriage would produce the line of the Davidic covenant, carrying God's promise forth even to Jesus himself.

The Christian's relationship to the future is now changed, not because we know the future—that is an attempt to control the future from the present—but because we know God will be there. We do not know *what* will be in the future, but we know *who* will be in the future. And that is a profound difference.

As Walter Benjamin pointed out, the Jews have always been "prohibited from investigating the future." Instead, their Torah as well as their prayers and psalms concentrates on *remembrance,* the remembrance of how God saved them from slavery, led them through the perils of the wilderness and kept them in the land of promise. This remembrance "stripped the future of its magic, to which all those succumb who turn to the soothsayers for enlightenment." But this remembrance of the presence and glory of God also works powerfully on the present. As Benjamin said, it does not leave time as a featureless vacuum waiting to be filled up with vagrant wishes and actions; instead "every second of time was the strait gate through which the Messiah might enter."[3]

Those who know Jesus is risen from the dead have discovered the future in a new way because they have remembered God's power over the dead past. They may be surprised; but they will not be taken by surprise. Neither the past nor the present will cause them to fear the future. Words that "never pass away" will overtake them, tossed up from somewhere deep within the human experience; they will come not sea-borne but Spirit-borne. They bear the message that these disciples also shall not be overcome, for "this generation will not pass away" until all is accomplished.

# 9

# The Crisis
# of the End Time
# & the Crisis
# of Our Time

*H*EAVEN AND EARTH WILL PASS AWAY, BUT MY WORDS WILL never pass away" (Mk 13:31). The fact that these words have endured down to our own time is of more than passing wonder. One can imagine unearthing an ancient stele engraved with these words as an ironic archaeological curiosity—rather like the monument left by Shelley's Ozymandias:

Look on my works, ye Mighty, and despair!

Nothing beside remains. Round the decay

Of that colossal wreck, boundless and bare

The lone and level sands stretch far away.

But the words of Jesus are as alive today as ever. They have survived the cynical best efforts of the Neros, the Julians and the Voltaires. For a time people believed the cynics; but each time a human community that ever had any acquaintance with these words comes on hard times, this gospel message comes to the surface, breaking on the shore of yet another shipwrecked generation.

## Signs of the Time
I need not predict anything at all to say that our own generation bears the marks of the end-time crisis. That is not to say, necessarily, that these are the end times. But it is to say that the kinds of contradictions and tensions that Jesus' teachings associated with the end of the world are as relevant to our own time as to any time in human memory.

What are the "signs of the times" that make these words peculiarly relevant today? Three observations will serve to underline the unique character of our own period in history.

1. *Our age is the first to experience a* universal *sense of living within an apocalyptic crisis.* On many occasions over the past two millennia Western people have been caught up in a strong *fin-de-siècle* state of mind. Certain calculations from the supposed beginning of the world, or from the advent of Christ, led to times of acute expectation. In a fascinating study of this phenomenon, *Century's End: A Cultural History of the Fin de Siècle,* Hillel Schwartz has noted that "each century's end since the year 1300 has borne ever more vivid witness" to peculiar end-of-the-era expectations. "Nightmares unconfirmed, utopian dreams unfulfilled, these do not fade forever from memory as a new century goes resolutely on." Instead they linger and escalate toward each successive century's end. "However disturbing it may seem to the historian accustomed to careful alignment of events in patient sequence, the jumps from one *fin de siècle* to the next have become cumulative." Then Schwartz says, "We have been preparing for the end of our century further in advance than people in any other century . . . [meaning that] those manichaean tensions common to the *fin de siècle* experience will be exaggerated in the 1990s."[1] These tensions are exaggerated even more, of course, by the fact that this is not only the end of a century but the end of the second millennium.

At the end of the twentieth century and the beginning of the twenty-first we have more to think about, however, than mathematical calculations. For such numbers, however significant they might seem, are referring primarily to a Christian tradition. What is happening to us today, though, involves a universal awareness of apocalyptic possibilities. Unlike former times, when only peoples of Christian lands had a sense of living within the scheme of historical expectations that Christianity had given rise to, today the world at large has reason to think about an end of history.

First, we are increasingly aware—and perhaps now so dreadfully aware that a kind of psychological denial has set in—that the choices we make and the problems we face are of a world-critical nature. For the first time in history, disturbances in the Middle East or Africa or East Europe send out shock waves to the farthest reaches of the globe. Before World War I the Balkans were a powder keg; before the next war Europe was a powder keg; today the world is a powder keg.

Distress on the streets of Los Angeles can affect Americans' readiness to respond to a crisis in East Africa. Yesterday Palestinians were killed in a mosque in Israel, today Jewish schoolboys were killed in New York. Violence no longer spreads in concentric circles outward; it arcs over the Atlantic, striking half a world away. Since the beginning of the twentieth century we have experienced the growing possibility that local feuds will draw the nations of the world into pitched battle. By the end of the twentieth century the sensitivity of world powers to remote political events has grown exponentially, and the consequences of a breakdown in the delicate balance of peace are horribly and dangerously multiplied.

Second, technology has vastly increased the scope of human action. Nuclear warheads on intercontinental missiles naturally come to mind. Midcentury, the medievalist and Catholic theologian Étienne Gilson was writing, "On the threshold of a new millennium, man has the proud conviction that the day is perhaps not far off when he himself will be able to explode the planet."[2] But the arsenal of apocalyptic warfare must be expanded now to include biological and chemical weapons of untold peril to the human family. Furthermore, destructive possibilities are not confined to warfare. Even peacetime attempts to "conquer" nature for the sake of a better life (that is, for more than we can possibly need or use), fulfilling Descartes's adage that we should become the "masters and possessors of nature," have added to our worries that we are rendering the earth barren and toxic. On every side we are in touch with the apocalyptic dangers of modern life.

Two thousand years ago, if the lights went out in Rome there was still somewhere to flee. Today there is nowhere else to go. Once the arena of public fortune and social disaster was Rome, or Jerusalem, or Athens. Today it is the world. Unlike any generation in the past, we are forced to think in terms of world consequences—and therefore of end-time consequences.

2. *While the technological nature of the crisis is impressive, it only serves to magnify the deeper* moral *nature of the human predicament.* We are faced with the dilemma that Bertrand de Jouvenel once described: "Every year we can do more and more, until now we can do more than ever before in history—yet what on earth shall we do?"[3] It is clear that the question "What shall we do?" touches no longer on the individual and community or even on the nation alone. Moral choices can affect the life of all humanity in a swift and comprehensive way. And while the moral strength of society and the character of individuals have always been important, we can now imagine conditions under which the capacity for making the right choice—or an occasion of moral blindness—can be critical to the continuation of life.

The book of Deuteronomy points out that to choose obedience to God is to choose life; disobedience leads to death. This ancient Hebrew theology of decisive life-or-death confrontation with the law has come down to our time more dramatically and decisively than ever. Not only does the choice of life over death affect us in cumulative and incremental ways, either assuring or denying the life of a community, but it may well come upon us as swiftly as the horsemen of the apocalypse. The awareness of that fact, along with a realistic assessment of humanity's tentative and feeble hold upon moral direction, gives rise, very justifiably, to thoughts of world crisis and apocalyptic consequences.

Just as moral choices are magnified in terms of consequences, the record of moral failure in the twentieth century has increased the foreboding. Hannah Arendt said that the real dangers posed by Hitler and Stalin, especially their mass murder and genocidal policies, did not disappear with their deaths and the collapse of their regimes. The evil that these regimes perpetrated upon their nations had been, in earlier times, unimaginable. As "solutions" to political problems they were not "possible," because they were far beyond the realm of anything considered morally acceptable. But the totalitarian regimes of this century have shown, in a way, that anything is possible. And even when the regimes themselves disappear—as they inevitably must—the "possibilities" are now imaginable. It is the solution itself that matters now, not the men who perpetrated this evil.

"The Nazis and the Bolsheviks," Arendt wrote, "can be sure that their factories of annihilation which demonstrate the swiftest solution to the problem of overpopulation, of economically superfluous and socially rootless human masses, are as much of an attraction as a warning." The policies, while still morally repulsive and condemned on every hand by people of conscience, have pushed back the limits of political possibilities. Wholesale state-sponsored abortions, medical experiments on human beings, euthanasia and even genocide are now no longer theoretical possibilities; they have become actual possibilities, live weapons waiting to be picked up when the occasion arises. These solutions, even while in relative disuse, said Arendt, "may well survive the fall of totalitarian regimes in the form of strong temptations which will come up whenever it seems impossible to alleviate political, social, or economic misery in a manner worthy of man."4

3. *The moral crisis of our time, while felt universally—that is, even outside the Christian communities—is strongly related to the progress of the gospel.* Late in the nineteenth century, the optimistic view of a gospel that was progressively elevating the moral climate of the world was standard fare. Adolf Harnack, the last of the great nineteenth-century liberal theologians, ended his book *What Is Christianity?* (originally lectures given at the University of Berlin in 1899-1900) with these words: "If we then look at the course of mankind's history, follow its upward development, and search, in strenuous and patient service, for the communion of minds in it, we shall not faint in weariness and despair, but become certain of God, of the God whom Jesus Christ called his Father, and who is also our Father."[5] There were no doubts about the upward development of humankind, nor of the part the Christian message played in it.

Decades later, historical optimism was still not dead, of course, but it was harder to come by. The world had witnessed two great wars and many smaller ones, claiming more lives than in any comparable period in history. There were also economic woes on a massive scale, the growth of totalitarian systems and mass murder on a scale never before known. Infamous place names like Auschwitz, Treblinka and Dachau and vast systems of slave and death camps in the Soviet Union and China did not argue persuasively for the "upward development" of humankind that Harnack spoke of so easily.

Historical optimism as a self-evident conviction has dimmed and almost died out since the early part of the twentieth century. However, a careful analysis of trends in human history can still yield the judgment that the Christian gospel has produced an inexorable movement that has had decisive effects in the moral self-image of humankind.

In René Girard's *The Scapegoat,* which I mentioned in chapter seven, he argues that in the course of history something critical has happened to an important social mechanism. That mechanism is the propensity of human societies for solving chaotic and insoluble social problems—the tensions that grip a community under the pressure of economic disruption, plagues, famines or other crises—by locating and persecuting a scapegoat. Giving numerous examples, Girard describes how a society in crisis loses its sense of order and decorum, making social interaction impossible and leading to chaos and fear. The identification of a scapegoat—for instance, a minority population—allows the community to arise from its paralysis and inaction and strike out, to take action against the crisis. The fact that the scapegoat is not responsible for the crisis makes no difference. The scapegoat becomes the focus of popular passions, and thus a renewed sense of community is born.

As late as the fourteenth century, it was still possible for large societies to identify (illogically) the Jewish population in Europe as responsible for the plagues and to persecute them, unconsciously and naively restoring community by identifying and killing the scapegoat. In the minds of all but the most acutely critical, these societies were ridding themselves of the cause of the problem. In actuality they were recovering a sense of order and community by joining in a common mission, even though the mission was the mass murder of innocent people.

But something clearly was happening, says Girard, to this age-old intuitive social mechanism. The persecutors began losing the freedom to act naively; society in general was becoming more aware of the injustice of their actions. More and more they had to disguise the mechanism itself and justify it with ideological or religious devices.

What had brought this profound change—this change in the way society viewed the acts of persecutors? It was the gospel of Christ. In this gospel one sees the actions of a community rallying in a crisis against a scapegoat. But this time we see the matter from the point of view of the innocent victim. Furthermore, we understand God as identified in and for and with the victim. So the gospel has ripped back the veil of secrecy surrounding the falsehood and violence of a society that maintains itself at the expense of victims. Formerly peace was bought at the price of the victim's blood. Now the victim and his story preclude the usual justification of the murder. Peace is bought at the price of the victim's blood now in another sense. The methods of murder and false accusation have been exposed and thus lose their capacity to reassemble magically the broken and chaotic elements of a society in turmoil.

These methods are now so exposed to censure in a world long tutored by the gospel that the story of the victim always has a chance of breaking out and destroying the persecutors' case, even when the persecutors are superior in number and resources.

"When the Gospels proclaim that Christ henceforth has taken the place of all victims, we only recognize grandiloquent sentimentality and piety," Girard points out, "whereas in the Gospel reference it is literally true." This is true because we have "learned to identify our innocent victims only by putting them in Christ's place."[6] Though cultures continued to live by allowing the verdict of collective guilt to fall first upon one group and then upon another, now the Lamb of God has taken the place of us all. The guilt has been lifted for all who believe and receive this gift, making it impossible now to pretend to restore peace through persecution and violence. It is injustice per se that is clearly opposed by God—not the injustice or guilt of select victims of society.

### The Cross, the Crisis and the Moral Order

Girard describes an inexorable progress—a progress that is ascribed to the gospel and empowered by the intervention of God. How, then, can one account for the sudden explosion of violence, social crises and potential for spiraling bloodshed in the twentieth century? Can it be that the gospel has indeed spread through the world with its message of peace and at the same time, and for the same reason, become an occasion for conflict? This might be true if we see the gospel as instigating a crisis in the moral order itself.

The vastness of a world crisis cannot be comprehended. But in the details of small crises we can begin to approach it. The gospel sets up a crisis in history just as it does in the life of an individual. I might successfully hide the truth of wrongdoing from myself for years. A habit of lying can be seen as only a cunning and clever strategy, with no thought given to the inevitable harm it does. Gossip can be merely lively, entertaining conversation, while I carefully conceal from myself the objective injury I am causing to another. A crisis occurs when I realize that a part of myself—the part that desires *not* to harm—is stirred by the realization of an undeniable truth, namely that I am doing harm by my lying and gossiping. The gospel introduces a crisis by shedding light on the truth of my behavior.

Consequently, as the gospel spreads it denies the world its cover of innocence and ambiguity. One must choose. The demands of the good and the true ring clear—too clear, in fact, to allow lies and violence as means of putting Good Causes into overdrive, or to allow the continuation of naive barbarian innocence.

I might continue my habits of lying and gossiping even after I recognize the truth. But I can no longer do it innocently. The truth has brought on an "identity crisis" of the gravest sort. Either I must give up my sin, or I must give up the desire not to do harm. If I insist on gossip, I can no longer do it without realizing what I am doing. I am consciously choosing evil, though I may work very hard at justifying the harm I am doing.

So in one way my lot is much worse. Before the truth dawned on me, I was at least consciously on the side of doing what is good; now if I continue to entertain friends or seek personal advantage in the same way, I must deliberately and consciously choose evil. To continue doing what I formerly did out of habit becomes now a deliberate choice, one that I can support only by more subtle forms of self-justification. If I am successful in escaping the pain of what I once did without a thought of evil, I can go even deeper into the mysteries of evildoing; my capacity to inflict pain on others increases because my skill at anesthetizing my own conscience has also increased.

In another way, however, I can say that my life is much improved, for to realize what is good is to have the opportunity to do it.

Either way, no one is permitted the luxury of ignorance. One must repent or, like Nietzsche, embrace evil as good, or, like the revolutionary Lenin, see violence as simply breaking eggs to make an omelet—a device that works so long as the eggs remain simple eggs and not human beings with faces and families.

## A World Split Apart

That is why some people can view the world as becoming better, moving to a higher moral plain and improving from age to age, while others are convinced it is rapidly going in the other direction. The truth is that we are moving in both directions at once, creating enormous and almost unbearable social tensions that beg for resolution. The crisis forces us to choose, and the choice is painful. We would prefer to put it off or to believe it is not there. We are ripe for repentance, but we are also ready for any messiah willing to promise us an easy way out.

But now, just as parasites and bacteria develop potent resistance to medicines intended to eradicate them, evil returns in a more cunning and virulent form. The straightforward barbarity of Europeans' killing Jews for "poisoning wells" during the bubonic plague of the fourteenth century is no longer possible. That is a kind of progress. But the barbarity of the twentieth century wears academic gowns and business suits, and if it discloses what it is doing at all, it speaks the esoteric language of some heretofore unknown moral struggle. Murders and persecutions in the twentieth century have reached a scale never known in the history of the world. At the same time the rhetoric of "human rights," moral outrage at the abuses of minorities and political dissidents, has never been more strongly voiced.

Just as agents of disease learn to disguise themselves in forms no longer recognizable to the systemic antibodies, programs of violence and enslavement wear the cloak of moral campaigns, espousing the noblest of intentions while spilling the blood of children in the streets. This is the truest paradox of the twentieth century. The pornography industry enslaves and wastes the lives of children but speaks the language of freedom of expression. The abortionist wears a surgeon's mask, and the medical profession, which in the public mind was long associated with mercy, provides cover for an industry based on blood money.

Yet it is the clarity with which good opposes evil that brings on this crisis and the strong temptation, as well as the extraordinary measures taken, to embrace evil as good. This must be why Paul spoke as if God were responsible for the "powerful delusion" of the last days "so that they will believe the lie" (2 Thess 2:11). The "powerful delusion" is occasioned precisely by the strongly felt need to act justly, thus giving rise to the urgency of justifying actions. One must choose between repentance and self-delusion. The choice has been forced upon us by God himself.

### The Crisis of Our Time and the Crisis of Jesus' Prophecies

To recapitulate these three points: The crisis of our time is more than symbolic and accidental (although popular attention will undoubtedly be drawn to the end of the millennium); it is technological and sociological in a very objective sese. Moreover, the crisis of our times is more than technological and sociological; it is moral. And finally, the crisis is more than moral; it is theological. It is a crisis brought on by the gospel's challenge to a world built on violence and falsehood.

How is it that the words of Jesus, when brought to bear on this multileveled world crisis, seem not to have faded in significance with the passing of time, like Ozymandias's inscription, but seem actually to be amplified and to become more potent than ever as the tensions of the modern world increase? I think we might begin to answer that question by taking note of a promise that is buried within these predictions of a world crisis and that seems to portend the end of the crisis. Mark (13:10) and Matthew (24:14) both recall the words that the gospel will be proclaimed to all the nations. Matthew's version explicitly says "and then the end will come."

What is the connection? Why is the intensity of the gospel associated with the worldwide spread of the gospel?

I knew a man who had stolen from his clients for a number of years. He was living an otherwise ordinary life. He was amiable, well-liked, confident and sought out as a community leader. Obviously the *doing* of evil—stealing money and breaking trusts—were not in themselves causing a crisis in this person's life. But when the truth came out, in the papers and on television, this man was immersed in the crisis of his life.

The nature of the gospel is that it throws us into crisis because it exposes us to the truth. Our sin becomes evident at least to ourselves, and we can no longer hide. So the spread of the gospel is met by increasing evasion, hypocrisy, violence and falsehood. It intensifies the human condition, because our rebellion becomes more and more intentional and desperate.

It is the very success of the gospel that invites worldwide condemnation from non-Christians, apostasy from within the church and finally widespread persecution. The world attempts to pull itself together again as it always has, by the assertion of power focused in violence against a scapegoat. In the end Christians become the focus of that last desperate attempt to use the age-old method of Satan: hatred and violence to galvanize people into a community of persecutors. The world wants stability and peace, but it will accept the illusion of peace based on the use of terror, intimidation and exclusion.

The fact that Christians will one day feel the cold stares and the hot fires of their persecutors is a major theme in Jesus' eschatological teachings. Indeed, through the centuries there have been many attempts to persecute Christians, and today there are fresh evidences of how the world can be enraged by the presence of the church.

Could it be that we are beginning to see a dividing of the ways: on the one hand, a church that realizes it cannot truly be the church of Jesus Christ while accommodating the increasing lawlessness of the world around it, and a larger society growing fiercely intolerant of Christians whose values insult its hedonism and its ambitions? Time will tell if this tension is a continuation of the world's story or the last chapter.

**Of Faithfulness and Hope**
The object of Jesus' teachings on the Mount of Olives, however, is to assure Christians that nothing can overcome them so long as they are faithful. As I finish this chapter, I am sitting in a beach house near Charleston. The sunroom overlooks the Atlantic Ocean and the approaches to the Charleston Harbor. Every so often a ship will appear, as if out of nowhere, on the horizon. Before long it is steaming close to shore toward the docks.

Though disturbing events may appear suddenly on our horizon, Jesus' teachings affirm that all events ultimately lead to his triumph. This is what John Greenleaf Whittier had in mind when he wrote these lines in 1867:

And so beside the silent sea
I wait the muffled oar;
No harm from him can come to me
On ocean or on shore.
I know not where his islands lift
Their fronded palms in air;
I only know I cannot drift
Beyond his love and care.

# 10

# Keeping Watch: Spiritual Initiative & World Crisis

*No one knows about that day or hour,*
*not even the angels in heaven, nor the Son,*
*but only the Father. Be on guard! Be alert!*
*You do not know when that time will come.*
*It's like a man going away: He leaves*
*his house and puts his servants in charge,*
*each with his assigned task, and tells*
*the one at the door to keep watch.*

*Therefore keep watch because you do not know*
*when the owner of the house will come back—*
*whether in the evening, or at midnight,*
*or when the rooster crows, or at dawn.*
*If he comes suddenly, do not let him*
*find you sleeping. What I say to you,*
*I say to everyone: "Watch!"*

*(MARK 13:32-37)*

*F*ATIGUE MAKES COWARDS OF US ALL," GOES AN OLD FOOT-
ball adage. Commands such as "Watch!" "Be on guard!" "Be alert!"
call for initiative against cowardice in the face of hard times.

Watching as a spiritual initiative is needed in a crisis when the
easiest choice may be desperately wrong and the right choice may be
desperately painful. To be alert here means to hold in view the time
of deliverance; it opposes the temptation to live with easy compromises, drowsily inattentive to the moral and spiritual perils of the passing world.

Two very different persons I have known exemplify this sort of alertness. While one was a poor and very unsophisticated schoolgirl and the other a highly skilled college professor, the memory of each serves as a model of how one may "wake up" and "watch" so that critical decisions are grounded in a fundamental truthfulness.

### The Eighth-Grader

The first incident comes from my teaching days in a rural North Carolina high school. When I think of that time I always remember Doretha, one of my students in an all-girl homeroom. That community was divided about evenly between people of African descent and Scotch-Irish-English descendants, and the former were generally poorer. But Doretha was poorer than most. I was her instructor in remedial reading and was well acquainted with the fact (known to all her classmates) that she could barely read.

That fact alone distinguished her from the other girls. Some of them were black, some white, none very wealthy; most were from middle-class homes. They were neat, clean, smiling and always as affable as you can expect teenagers to be. In the midst of this swirl of sociability sat Doretha, with ill-fitting clothes awkwardly arranged on a squat, roundish frame, looking on the rest with sullen eyes. Her infrequent comments were usually inappropriate, a little belligerent for someone who hadn't been attacked, or even spoken to—and they were usually ignored.

But there is another reason she stands out in my memory. A small gesture that she has likely forgotten has brought her to mind a dozen or more times over the years since. This gesture captured the attention of a whole gaggle of not-too-serious teenage girls and caused us all to wake up to a certain reality.

The federal court rulings on prayer in public schools had not yet made an impact in rural eastern North Carolina. Every morning several homeroom classes, including mine, opened with a brief devotional and the pledge of allegiance. I had asked that any girl who wanted to participate sign up for a particular day in the month. Each day some-one would have the devotional reading. Usually the girls would bring something from home—a devotional book or a column from the church paper. Many times they simply selected a passage from Scripture.

One month Doretha signed up for the devotional reading. No one said anything, but there were knowing glances around the class. *Doretha!* they thought; we *all* wondered, *What can she do?* While she was practically illiterate—a slow reader even with private tutoring—she was absolutely paralyzed and speechless if called on to read in public.

The day before her turn came I thought it best to ask if she was seriously intending to carry through. "Yes suh," she said. I should have known: she was nothing if not serious.

The next morning I approached her again, wanting to make her retreat as easy as possible. I could only guess at the courage it took for her to do this. What prompted her, I do not know; perhaps it was the sheer indignity of always being intimidated by the chorus of bright, well-dressed peers. But she insisted she was ready. The other girls glanced uneasily at her, half curious and half anxious that she would commit a great blunder so that they would have to sit looking at the floor, pretending no one was putting her backwardness on public display.

"Are you ready, Doretha?"

"Yes."

"Come on up."

Unlike many teenagers, who twitter and gyrate when they stand up to speak, she might have grown out of the floor where she stood. Looking somewhat shorter and stockier than when she sat among the other girls, Doretha had a strange dignity in her bearing; her gaze was level and serious. Most surprising, however, there was nothing—not a book, not a scrap of paper—in her hand. With only a moment's hesitation, she repeated from memory John 3:16: "For God so loved

the world that he gave his only begotten Son . . ." Her voice had a
sincerity and directness that we had not heard before. Somehow this
word had stayed with her, captured in her memory, because it meant
something to her that *someone* loved her that much.

A curious stillness settled over the class. I couldn't help noticing
their faces. There was a kind of awe in them—the way we look when
seeing something we never expected to see, at least not where we've
found it. Perhaps they had never really seen Doretha before that moment, and then, just for a fleeting moment, it crossed their minds that
something wonderfully extravagant had been done for someone who,
to them, was an utter outcast—poor, illiterate, unsociable Doretha.
There was no more impressive devotional all year long.

This was a small sign of a certain kind of power: the power of an
awakening to something right in our midst.

**The Professor**
The other example is from almost the precise opposite end of the
social spectrum. Dr. Gerhart Niemeyer of Notre Dame University was
brilliant, confident, sophisticated, well-known and respected. He had
little in common, at first glance, with a poor Carolina schoolchild in
a remedial reading class. Except this one thing: in the classroom one
could sense something extra, and something quite powerful, in the way
he taught. And this kind of strength, I think, lay very close to what
Doretha tapped into that morning in front of twenty-some eighth-
graders. Only here, a small room full of graduate students turned the
pages of difficult philosophical texts and labored to understand new
ideas.

When I first came into the seminar on "the reconstruction of political theory," we were assigned a reading of Henri Bergson's *The Two
Sources of Morality and Religion,* a work of great importance in
twentieth-century social philosophy. Bergson's method lay so entirely
outside the ordinary way of thinking that the concepts came to us

slowly and only with conscious efforts to reflect critically on some of our basic mental habits.

Professor Niemeyer worked to help us "see" the text, going beyond a superficial reading. At first I could understand nothing. Then little islands of thought began to form; I understood some related concepts on this subject and that, but the whole thesis, and the real importance of Bergson's argument, eluded me. Nevertheless, I noticed that the hour and half of the seminar went by swiftly. The professor lifted out critical parts of the text; he prodded us to express the ideas differently, to draw conclusions, to extrapolate a line of thought—even to see other ways of thinking critically. He gave illustration after illustration: stories from literature, experiences, lines from poetry. He drove us deeper and deeper. He was forming new habits in our thinking. He had his eyes on something we could not yet see.

The seminar members came from varied backgrounds. Some were Notre Dame graduates, some not. Some were Catholic, many were not. One or two had grown up outside the United States. A few were from the East Coast, a couple of us were from the South, and the rest were Midwesterners. One student would soon go to Johns Hopkins to study international relations; another young man from Detroit would soon go to law school. One was an air force officer; another was entering academic publishing. We had broad interests and different ways of going at a subject. But gradually our thoughts began to circulate around a common center—and for a significant period of time we did not know precisely what was the nature of that "center." The picture had not yet come clear. We only knew there was a teacher among us who "saw" something that we did not yet see.

What intrigues me even today, more than a decade later, is the level of tension, or anticipation, Dr. Niemeyer was able to generate among students. We strained for something, not fully grasping it, yet not expecting to grasp it immediately. It was not information we were being given—not something to drop easily into our minds without changing anything therein. What we were straining after was a new perspective, a way of seeing ordinary things in a new light. This learning was not like new furnishings added to the old; it was something that was acting upon us. We were being changed.

As we continued to read Bergson, suddenly those islands of thought began to grow together—a world was created anew. In the seminar our conversation began to be animated by this "thought," this new habit of seeing. Bergson's book suddenly became a floodlight illuminating some of the dark recesses of life. As we sat there with our guide, I could only have described our experience as an *emotion*. And the sustained effort needed in order to bring us through to this point where we could "see" what Bergson was saying had been conveyed to us by Professor Niemeyer. He generated and transmitted to us a kind of emotional attachment to something that, in the beginning, he alone among us was able to see.

Every really good teacher I have ever known has had this ability. It consists of a loyalty—I might almost say a "love"—toward something that is of such transcending value and importance that it is capable of making demands on life, of changing life. Moreover, this relationship between teacher and the object of his or her thought, so charged with emotion, turns the classroom experience into an adventure, a seeking after something not yet seen, and a knowledge that once it is found our minds and hearts will no longer be the same.

In Jacob Needleman's remarkable little book *The Heart of Philosophy,* he makes a similar point about Socrates. Why was he so important in the life of Western philosophy? Needleman asks. He left no writings. We know him mainly through the dialogues of Plato and the memoirs of Xenophon. But we also know that the *effect* of his personality, his teaching and his life quest are immeasurable. What was the nature of that effect? What was Socrates' power to transform the lives and thinking of his world, and of worlds long after him? Needleman describes this effect as *eros*—the power of love. Socrates was able to "kindle *eros,* a longing for being."[1] He had a loving loyalty to something greater than himself, something outside himself, something of transcendent value. And this love of that which was greater than individual, isolated life, greater even than the life of the community, greater than the world itself—this love awakened a hunger in the hearts of some who knew him.

Professor Niemeyer led students not to his opinions but into the text that lay before them. His teaching was not simply method, it was a fundamental truthfulness.

Doretha, on one occasion, gave her classmates a glimpse of something more than her well-known petulance and irritability. She gave them a vision of how she stood before God—and consequently of how *they* stood.

Watchfulness always has this quality about it. It centers not on the self but on something greater and something outside. Its power is in its honesty, its reflection of the truth outside the observer.

### The Truth of the Watcher

We can also say, therefore, that Jesus' admonition—"Watch! Be on guard! Be alert!"—means to be truthful. Jesus urges disciples to face the crisis, to make the difficult choice when they discern that that is the right choice. The inattentive one, the one overcome with fatigue and drowsiness, will choose the easy way, the way of drifting undisturbed into sleep—and into death.

It is moral stamina that Jesus calls for, made possible by constant watching. If we make the right choice in a crisis, it must come from the habit of making those more difficult choices daily. "Watching" is then a habit of truthfulness. It is being truthful about the world and about oneself. It is being honest before God. It is a disposition against denial and therefore against being taken by surprise when the truth and falsity of things come suddenly upon us. Jesus will not take by surprise those who are watching for him. False wishes and deceit will undermine only those who insist on believing lies.

Inattentiveness does not come from an inability to see but from an *unwillingness*. We do not desire to see, and therefore we are blind to what is true.

Isaiah was commissioned to say to the people that *this* is what leads to their ruin:

Be ever hearing, but never understanding;
    be ever seeing, but never perceiving.
make the heart of this people calloused;
    make their ears dull
    and close their eyes.
Otherwise they might see with their eyes,
    hear with their ears,
    understand with their hearts,
and turn and be healed. (Is 6:9-10)

Here is the prelude to ruin—utter ruin—Isaiah was told. "How long?" he asks. Until the full effect of the blind eyes, inattentive ears, and dull hearts are known:

Until the cities lie ruined
    and without inhabitant,
until the houses are left deserted,
    and the fields ruined and ravaged. (6:11)

The whole prophetic movement, the true core of Israel's religion, was marked by a moral insight into the nature of God, carried forward by those who "saw." The more ancient term for a prophet was *rō'eh,* or "seer"—one who sees what others miss, one whose eyes are open. That describes who they were, and it explains their power.

Once G. K. Chesterton drew attention to a peculiar feature of medieval Christian art, which depicted the Christian saint so differently from the depiction of Gautama in Buddhist art. While the reposing or seated Buddha rests with his eyes closed, Chesterton noted, the Christian saint's body may be "wasted to its crazy bones, but his eyes are frightfully alive."[2]

Like Chesterton, I believe there is an important clue here. In the Gospels we find Jesus opening the eyes of the blind. "Are you the one who was to come, or should we expect someone else?" John the Baptist asks. Jesus sends him word: "Go back and report to John . . . the blind receive sight" (Lk 7:22).

## The Need for Truth in Critical Days

In these teachings the command to watch responds to a crisis and cannot fully be understood apart from the warning of a crisis. There are three reasons that the command to watch is particularly appropriate to the warning of a crisis:

1. It means facing pain and mortality (truthfulness, not denial).

2. It means declaring loyalty to a higher vision of life (expectancy, not complacency).

3. It gains the moral advantage of a new perspective (making possible active love rather than reactive self-defense).

Let's look at these one at a time, noting the peculiarly fitting way in which Jesus' admonition to watch responds to the moral requirements of a person, or a world, facing crisis.

*1. It means facing pain and mortality (truthfulness, not denial).* A certain school of medical thought, I understand, believes that pain-relieving medicine actually retards the body's capacity for dealing with pain. If that is true, it certainly parallels the social effects of not facing painful truths. Society prefers the narcotic of refusing to face painful situations, believing that by refusing reality it is affirming life. For half a century at least, the post-Christian West has been bingeing on "life-affirming" philosophies. These include the cult of "faith in our own positive attitudes," the psychology of the Yankee trader. But they also go back to the most deeply rooted of modern myths—one so deeply rooted we seldom recognize it as a myth: the belief in a general, inevitable *progress,* which is really belief in a kind of secular immortality. These narcotics have allowed us to march to the edge of a cultural and social abyss without so much as hesitating to consider the warnings of thinkers who are otherwise much admired.

An example is Walker Percy, the late novelist, who commented on the paradox of the twentieth-century American's bent for life-affirming pronouncements—self-actualization, self-expression, self-improvement, self-esteem. At the same time, he said, no other century has been more "death-dealing in its actions." Then he wrote, "It is the century of the love of death."

I am not just talking about Verdun or the Holocaust or Dresden or Hiroshima. I am talking about a subtler form of death, a death in life, of people who seem to be living lives which are good by all sociological standards and yet who somehow seem more dead than alive. Whenever you have a hundred thousand psychotherapists talking about being life-affirming and a million books about life-enrichment, you can be sure there is a lot of death around.[3]

The seriousness and the honesty of facing pain, on the other hand, have a bracing effect. To face pain is to acknowledge reality, to awake and be strengthened rather than to be drugged with the anesthetic of wishes. Intuitively when we are faced with the honest picture of our situation—our limits, our mortality and our pain—we begin to think we are onto something. Truth is the prerequisite of hope.

The words of Jesus, then, so undervalued in our day (though they are sometimes exploited by sensationalists), are strong medicine, but definitely not anesthetic.

*2. It means declaring loyalty to a higher vision of life (expectancy, not complacency).* Earlier I mentioned that the Chinese character for "crisis" is composed of two words—one meaning danger and the other opportunity. The danger faced at the end time, like the dangers faced in Jesus' own time, will bear the possibilities of redemption. Danger will beckon courage. Betrayal will make loyalty a precious commodity. Truth will shine like a star in the darkness of a deceitful world. Every evil will increase the longing for virtue, just as darkness makes the eyes strain for light and a strange land increases the longing for home.

Jesus' loyalty seems the more remarkable in that he was betrayed. His steadfastness in the truth stands in contrast to Caiaphas's reliance on deceit, and his courage stands in stark contrast to Pilate's cowardice. "If I be lifted up," he said, "all men will be drawn to me." And so they were: on the cross he was lifted above his betrayers, his false friends and his enemies. Because of that, the world beheld him.

One day, beyond the crisis of this day, they will behold him again. It is that truth that makes every crisis not only bearable but even hopeful.

*3. It gains the moral advantage of a new perspective (making possible active love rather than reactive self-defense).* A Greek philosopher said that if he had a lever long enough and *a place to stand,* he could move the world. The words Jesus spoke on Mount Olivet provide a place to stand when the world seems a very unreliable place. With John Mason Neale we know that

Our hopes are weak, our fears are strong,

Thick darkness blinds our eyes;

Cold is the night; Thy people long

That Thou, their Sun, wouldst rise.

In this last part of Mark 13, the lies, the persecutions and the wars have given way to the disasters of nature. "At that time . . . the sun will be darkened and the moon will not give its light; the stars will fall from the sky, and the heavenly bodies will be shaken" (vv. 24-25). The calamities of nature have a way of demonstrating just how small and uncertain are human designs—even if they are the designs of war and violence. The great touting of humanity and the thundering of its engines of war fall silent when the ground itself gives way and the light of heaven fails.

Once in eastern North Carolina my wife and I, along with thousands of others, witnessed a total eclipse of the sun. On a perfectly clear summer afternoon, the disk of the moon silently blotted out the disk of the sun. What surprised us was the silence.

I had not noticed until then that our environment (a university campus in a rural area) was alive with sounds—birds, frogs, insects, children playing. Then everything stopped, standing silent, awestruck, at the most fleeting display of the sun's failing light.

The only other time I recall that kind of effect was when, a few years ago, I stood one night gazing at the sky, a sky just cleared and still in the eye of Hurricane Hugo. Twenty-four hours earlier, thoughts of tests to grade, students to meet and a point I needed to argue in the curriculum committee had crowded most other things out of my mind and off my schedule. But in that moment of silence, amid the devastation of nature's monster of a hurricane, those matters seemed a world away, blown like straws before the wind.

One moment we are caught up in an all-consuming human struggle. The next moment nature misses a tick and all that is blown flat; we dismiss it from our minds. The sun blinks, and we fall silent. The earth shudders, and our lofty ambitions crumble.

The text reminds us of how quickly we realize that something looms greater than the human predicament. And if we see there only nature, and if it too is unsteady, where do we find a place to stand? What is truly permanent, if anything? What can endure? These are questions that immediately and involuntarily come to mind. And they are why this apocalyptic imagery affects us so deeply.

Ancient Jews under persecution invented apocalyptic literature. It was highly symbolic and often involved strange otherworldly conflicts. But more important, it was highly dualistic in its point of view. That means that sometimes it pictured a new, transformed world of the future and incorporated principally an eschatological vision. At other times, in what is known as ascension apocalyptic, the prophet would be elevated to a new plane of existence, to the realm of God and the angels. Our one true example of this kind of literature in the New Testament is the book of Revelation. Its dualism can be seen in both the futuristic schema of the whole book and in the ascending of John to the throne room of heaven in chapter 4.

To modern people the intensity of this dualistic vision is so strange that we easily dismiss it. But the achievement and the great value of apocalyptic consist in its ability to suggest a new and greater arena of activity. In other words, in a time of persecution and hardship it gives creative and prophetic expression to a *new perspective*. In Revelation, for instance, John is lifted up to the throne room of heaven, where he sees the fate of martyrs in a different light. In this vision we find a strong contrast to what Christians were actually experiencing at that time. On earth one would see only violence, death, grief, loss, children orphaned and families impoverished. In Revelation the martyrdom on earth becomes a reign with Christ in glory, as the persecuted join in the praise of God the Father and rejoice in final victory.

**The Secret of the Second Coming**
I believe that any unprejudiced look at Jesus' words on the last things will tell us that he was teaching his disciples how to *live* by teaching them what to *expect*. They are, at heart, ethical teachings—not in the sense of imposing a law or giving a moral admonition, but in the sense of raising intense expectations that demanded something of the disciples, even in the face of the most daunting opposition and the most painful circumstances. The secret that lies at the heart of existence, and that will one day be as clear and evident as the dawn, is that God's intention to do good for us will not fail. If we rightly understand it, every particle of the universe, every turn in history and every wind of circumstance helps to accomplish God's purpose. And that purpose is altogether good.

Returning to Doretha for a moment, imagine the crisis of an adolescent girl attempting to find her place in life against the disadvantages of being quite poor and not very attractive in the midst of schoolmates who must seem to have every possible social advantage. Then imagine the possibility that God has planted in her a strong awareness of something—an awakening to the reality that she need not struggle for acceptance, for she has been given it; she need not justify her existence, for its justification rests in the loving act of an Almighty God. Just imagine that this awakening to a new awareness of her self before God takes root and grows in her life.

What might begin to happen? I think we would see the emerging of a new life—one capable of being lifted above the din of the struggle for self-preservation and self-justification. Put another way, it would be a life capable of seeing others clearly, no longer as contenders in the unending struggle for a place in the sun but as objects of God's love along with her. It would be a life freed to participate in that love. It would be a life that "watches," not out of a need for self-defense but out of an expectation of seeing God at any moment.

Ultimately, unless this conviction about life is true, we find ourselves having to choose, whether consciously or not, between two other assumptions. One is that life is a struggle and each person will find only the good that he or she wrests from the jaws of fate through talent and striving or through blind luck. The other view is that life is ultimately futile and pointless. No matter how many prizes we win, they are eventually covered up by the dust of death, lost forever in a meaningless universe. The "preacher" of Ecclesiastes gives eloquence to this choice: "So I hated life, because the work that is done under the sun was grievous to me. All of it is meaningless, a chasing after the wind" (Eccles 2:17).

But if the gospel is true—that is, if good news must prevail and evil ultimately will fail—then we face life with a kind of freedom and confidence that are otherwise impossible. There is a good reason the church symbolized the virtue of hope with an anchor. We may be tossed about by the restless waves of world history and the uncertainties of personal existence, but if at the same time we are firmly tied to a future that cannot be disturbed or changed in any essential way, the anchor of hope keeps us from being swept away.

We watch because we believe in deliverance and base every thought and action on that belief. So "when these things begin to take place, stand up and lift up your heads, because your redemption is drawing near" (Lk 21:28).

# Notes

**Chapter 1: Facing the Question**

[1] At this point I am relying on a book I read during those days: Norman Cohn, *The Pursuit of the Millennium* (New York: Oxford University Press, 1970), pp. 127-47.

[2] Ibid., p. 136.

[3] Ibid., pp. 223-80.

[4] Rudolf Bultmann, "New Testament and Mythology," in *Kerygma and Myth: A Theological Debate,* ed. Hans Werner Bartsch (New York: Harper & Row, 1961), pp. 1-2.

[5] Ibid., p. 5.

**Chapter 2: Not One Stone Left**

[1] Joseph Bonsirven, *Palestinian Judaism in the Time of Jesus Christ* (New York: Holt, Rinehart and Winston, 1964), p. 121.

[2] Flavius Josephus, *Antiquities of the Jews,* in *The Life and Work of Flavius Josephus,* trans. William Whitson (New York: Holt, Rinehart and Winston, n.d.), p. 474.

[3] *The Letter of Aristeas* 92-94, cited in Bonsirven, *Palestinian Judaism,* pp. 120-21.

**Chapter 5: The Coming Judgment**

[1] "Infant Holy, Infant Lowly" (Polish carol, trans. Edith M. G. Reed, 1925).

[2] "Lo, He Comes with Clouds Descending" (Charles Wesley, 1758).

[3] Quoted from Aristotle's *Nicomachean Ethics,* in Abraham Heschel, *The Prophets* (New York: Harper & Row, 1962), 2:4 n.

[4]Heschel, *The Prophets,* 2:4.

[5]Ibid., 2:5.

[6]Ibid.

[7]Cited as Marcionite arguments by Tertullian *Adversus Marcionem* 1.6; 2.11.25; and *De Idolatria* 5; and by Hippolytus *Refutatio omnium haeresium* 7.30; in Heschel, *The Prophets,* 2:80.

[8]Heschel, *The Prophets,* 2:80, quoting E. F. Micka, *The Problem of Divine Anger in Arnobius and Lactantius* (Washington: n.p., 1943), p. 30.

[9]Heschel, *The Prophets,* 2:83.

[10]Elie Wiesel, *Night,* trans. Stella Rodway (New York: Avon Books, 1960), pp. 74-76.

## Chapter 6: The False Messiah

[1]Nathaniel Hawthorne, *The Blithedale Romance* (1852; Sears ed.), chap. 9; quoted in Melvin Lasky, *Utopia and Revolution* (Chicago: University of Chicago Press, 1976), p. 73.

[2]Hawthorne, *Blithedale Romance,* quoted in ibid., pp. 73-74.

[3]Bernard McGinn in *The Encyclopedia of Religion,* ed. Mircea Eliade (New York: Macmillan, 1987), p. 323.

[4]Hans Jonas, *The Gnostic Religion* (Boston: Beacon, 1958), p. 103.

[5]Irenaeus *Against Heresies* 1.23.2-3; quoted in Jonas, *The Gnostic Religion,* p. 108.

[6]See A. J. Conyers, *The Eclipse of Heaven: Rediscovering the Hope of a World Beyond* (Downers Grove, Ill.: InterVarsity Press, 1992).

[7]Samuel J. Andrews, *Christianity and Anti-Christianity in Their Final Conflict* (Chicago: Bible Institute Colportage Association, 1898), pp. 137-38.

[8]Ibid., pp. 262-63.

## Chapter 7: The Holy Spirit & the Last Days

[1]*Scapegoat mechanism* is a term René Girard uses in several writings, but it finds its fullest explication in *The Scapegoat,* trans. Yvonne Freccero (Baltimore: Johns Hopkins University Press, 1986).

## Chapter 8: Remembrance of Things to Come

[1]Tertullian *Apology* 42, in *The Ante-Nicene Fathers,* ed. Alexander Roberts and James Donaldson (Grand Rapids, Mich.: Eerdmans, 1989), 3:49.

[2]Robert Frost, "The Road Not Taken," in *Collected Poems of Robert Frost*

(Cutchogue, N.Y.: Buccaneer Books, 1986), p. 131.

³Walter Benjamin, *Illuminations,* trans. Harry Zohn (New York: Schocken Books, 1969), p. 264.

**Chapter 9: The Crisis of the End Time & the Crisis of Our Time**

¹Hillel Schwartz, *Century's End: A Cultural History of the Fin de Siècle from the 990s through the 1990s* (New York: Doubleday, 1990), p. 11.

²Quoted in ibid., p. 8.

³This question as posed by Bertrand de Jouvenel was related to me in conversation by Jürgen Moltmann in 1986.

⁴Hannah Arendt, *The Origins of Totalitarianism* (New York: Harcourt Brace Jovanovich, 1973), p. 459.

⁵Adolf Harnack, *What Is Christianity?* trans. Bailey Saunders (New York: Harper & Row, 1957), p. 301.

⁶René Girard, *The Scapegoat,* trans. Yvonne Freccero (Baltimore: Johns Hopkins University Press, 1986), p. 202.

**Chapter 10: Keeping Watch**

¹Jacob Needleman, *The Heart of Philosophy* (San Francisco: Harper & Row, 1986), p. 35.

²G. K. Chesterton, *Orthodoxy* (Garden City, N.Y.: Doubleday, 1959), p. 131.

³Walker Percy, "Novel Writing in an Apocalyptic Time," in *Signposts in a Strange Land,* ed. Patrick Samway (New York: Farrar, Straus & Giroux, 1991), p. 162.